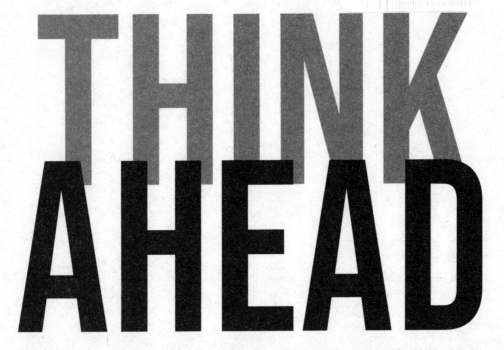

THINK AHEAD

THE POWER OF PRE-DECIDING FOR A BETTER LIFE

WORKBOOK | 15 LESSONS

CRAIG GROESCHEL

WITH DUDLEY DELFFS

HarperChristian
Resources

CONTENTS

PART 6: I WILL BE CONSISTENT

PART 7: I WILL BE A FINISHER

INTRODUCTION

Today's decisions determine who we become tomorrow.

Whether we like it or not, our lives become the sum of the daily decisions we make. Sure, some of our big decisions seem like more obvious turning points or forks in the road toward the direction our lives take. But before we face those apparently life-changing choices, we have made thousands, perhaps millions, of small, seemingly mundane and inconsequential choices that have brought us to those big decisions.

Each of our smallest decisions, from what to eat for breakfast (or whether to eat breakfast) to how we will get to work to when we will binge-watch the next season of our favorite show, shapes us into who we are. Basically, every choice you make as well as the ones you choose not to make casts a vote toward who and what controls your life. Enjoying a fruitful, successful life is not based on a few big decisions—whether to marry, where to live, which job to take—as much as it's built on the sculpture chiseled by the small cuts and chips made by your daily choices.

Knowing the impact of all our choices reinforces the importance of looking ahead and considering the consequences. When we think ahead, we can envision the way our choices begin to align and form patterns that reveal who we're becoming. Thinking ahead, we glimpse the way our good decisions have a compound benefit on our lives even as our bad decisions send us down a dead-end street.

Just consider a bad decision you've made. You probably didn't plan for it to become a launching pad for other bad decisions, but sometimes we land on a slippery slope where we try to regain lost ground only to discover we're even further from where we want to be. Suddenly, your decision to give in to temptation and allow an exception just this once becomes something you do again. And then again. And suddenly it becomes a habit spreading collateral damage in your life. What started as a splurge or one-time indulgence leads to an unhealthy habit or addiction that results in hiding it and lying about it to others. One bad choice permitted you to make others until suddenly they've multiplied and forced you to face their painful consequences.

On the other hand, one good decision often begets the next good decision. You experience the power of creating a pattern that's healthy, constructive, and positive. You find it easier to resist making bad decisions because you don't want to undo the progress you've made or stop enjoying the benefits of your good choices. Soon you're thinking less about which choice to make because you've already decided how to keep your momentum in this powerful, positive direction.

So, based on where you are right now, do you like where your decisions are taking you? Do you feel good about who you are and where you are in life? Do you believe God is pleased with your current direction?

Regardless of where you are, you probably would like to either change the way you've been making decisions in your life or continue making good choices in a more consistent, intentional way. And that's what this workbook is all about. To enhance your reading and application of *Think Ahead*, this guide can help you personalize and prioritize your new method of making decisions. Knowing you will *decide now* what you will *do later* can become a profound spiritual tool for re-ordering your life in a way that pleases and glorifies God and allows you to enjoy becoming who you were meant to be.

Deciding ahead of time what you will do is not as simple, of course, as it sounds. Among the numerous obstacles and challenges that get in our way, three stand out: being overwhelmed by options and possible outcomes; being afraid to make wrong choices with uncertain outcomes; and allowing emotions to interfere with your logic and clarity. These can be overcome, though, by owning and implementing seven life-defining pre-decisions that provide a foundation for success:

1. I will be ready.
2. I will be devoted.
3. I will be faithful.
4. I will be an influencer.
5. I will be generous.
6. I will be consistent.
7. I will be a finisher.

Are you ready to choose who you will become?

To live the life you want to live?

To enjoy peace, passion, and purpose as you honor God?

Then it's time to reconsider how you make decisions.

No matter your circumstances, your age, or your stage of life, it's not too late to change course and choose your life's direction. The quality of your decisions *will* determine the quality of your life. The choices you make today *will* determine the story you tell tomorrow.

You will never fall behind where you want to be if you're willing to *think ahead*!

PART 1

I WILL BE
READY

No one deliberately plans on making careless, impulsive decisions that lead to pain, injury, disappointment, shame, and broken relationships. But when you fail to prepare for how to defend your weaknesses and overcome temptation ahead of time, you set yourself up to fail. You must be prepared when temptations come knocking. As you begin preparing for future temptations, you can choose to eliminate many of them by deciding right now how to remove yourself from the front line of battle. By pre-deciding that you will be ready, you prepare for victory with a firm foundation of truth. Here are the key principles you will learn in part 1:

- No one plans to mess up their life—but they also don't plan *not* to.
- It is not a sin to be tempted; it becomes a sin when you decide to act on temptation.
- By pre-deciding to be ready when you face temptation, you take a stand against the enemy.
- You tend to think you're stronger and can handle more than you actually can.
- Making up your mind how to respond before the moment of temptation arrives helps you move the line between you and what tempts you.
- You have the power to resist future temptations by choosing to eliminate them right now.
- Boundaries based on God's guidelines are not limiting—they're freeing.

MOVE THE LINE

*Instead of being unwise, unaware, and unalert, we are
making up our minds to be ready for the moment of temptation.
We are pre-deciding to move the line.*[1]

CRAIG GROESCHEL

Erica Calderon, a thirty-something mother of two young daughters in Phoenix, lost eighty-five pounds by "moving the line" in two strategic areas of temptation.[2] She realized that coming home at the end of a long day left her tired and hungry and willing to eat whatever was available. So she began doing herself a favor by planning and cooking dinner ahead of time. Throwing together a nutritious meal left to simmer in a slow cooker all day, Erica knew she had something healthy and delicious already waiting for her. She moved the line of satisfying her appetite with fast food or whatever was available by making sure something better was ready.

Erica's other method of moving the line was to not watch television in her kitchen. "Sometimes, I'll go upstairs to watch my shows instead of sitting in the living room, which is attached to the kitchen. That way, I'm less likely to scavenge." Erica knew that adding distance would make it less likely for her to stop her television viewing and start snacking.[3]

Sounds like an obvious, commonsense approach, right? Nonetheless, whether with healthy eating or other lifestyle choices, we often fail to anticipate where the line between a good choice and a less-than-good choice falls. So, we end up feeling our way toward that boundary, often going over the line and wondering why we couldn't stop ourselves.

When we're drawn to something or someone, we often ignore the line until it's too late. We see how close we can dance on the edge between wrong and right. We know we don't want to yield to temptation, but we skate along the border, assuming we can control ourselves and rely on willpower to pull us back. Rarely, however, do we find the strength to resist. Instead, we must learn to move the line so that we can keep a healthy distance between ourselves and what tempts us.

- How do Erica's strategies for healthier eating habits strike you? Can you relate to her way of anticipating her needs ahead of time to provide better options?

- When have you wanted to change a habit or pattern of behavior in your life most recently? What choices did you make to help you attain your goal?

- How difficult is it for you to look ahead at the consequences of your choices and work your way back to the decision right in front of you? What complicates your ability to see the connection between present decisions and future success?

- When have you moved a line by anticipating your threshold of temptation and intentionally distanced yourself? Did this help you resist temptation?

EXPLORING GOD'S WORD

As you explore how to make better choices by pre-deciding, you will find it helpful to consider your usual decision-making process and the default ways you often respond to stress, tension, conflict, and temptation. You know you want to make good choices that honor God, help you grow, and contribute to your overall physical, emotional, mental, and spiritual health. Knowing what you should do, however, is rarely the issue. Instead of focusing simply on what you know would be good for you, it's helpful to identify what interferes with your ability to act on what you know.

Three of the most powerful categories blocking your ability to think ahead and make good decisions include feeling overwhelmed by too many options, yielding to fear about making bad choices that result in painful consequences, and allowing other emotions to disrupt your decision-making ability. Knowing how these obstacles get in your way allows you to strategize ways to think ahead and remove them before you're in the heat of the what-do-I-do moment.

We will explore each of these three barriers and how to overcome them in more detail, but before your deep dive into decision-making, allow yourself to take a deep breath, calm your mind, and still yourself before God. He knows your heart better than you do and wants to help you grow and be the divine image-bearer he created you to be. Inviting his presence into your process makes a huge difference in your perspective and attitude. With this goal in mind, make the words of the psalmist your prayer:

> [1] You have searched me, Lord,
>   and you know me.
> [2] You know when I sit and when I rise;
>   you perceive my thoughts from afar.
> [3] You discern my going out and my lying down;
>   you are familiar with all my ways. . . .
>
> [23] Search me, God, and know my heart;
>   test me and know my anxious thoughts.
> [24] See if there is any offensive way in me,
>   and lead me in the way everlasting.

PSALM 139:1–3, 23–24

- What word or phrase stands out or speaks to you in this passage? Why does it resonate?

- Why does the psalmist begin by acknowledging, "You have searched me, LORD," and then closes by asking, "Search me, God, and know my heart"? How does inviting God into your process help you become more self-aware?

- What thoughts or emotions stir inside you as you reflect on how intimately God knows you? Guilt? Shame? Relief? Gratitude? Something else?

- What do you believe has contributed to most of the bad decisions you've made in the past? Why?

EMBRACING THE TRUTH

Asking God to search you and know your heart also increases your ability to see your weaknesses and areas of vulnerability. Not only does the Holy Spirit allow you to see your struggles beyond what's visible to your eyes, but you also surrender your defenses and humbly face what's true about how you've arrived at where you are in your life right now.

Your past mistakes, the decisions you regret, and your emotional baggage don't have to prevent you from making better choices and from experiencing positive change. You can ask God to help you decide now what you will do later, when circumstances blindside you or emotions overwhelm you. With God's help and guidance, your choices from this point forward can be different from the choices made by default in the past.

It's easy to make false assumptions and reach faulty conclusions based on your history of not always making the best decisions you long to make. You might get stuck in your head, telling yourself, "Yeah, it's always been this way. I always seem to repeat the same mistakes. I'm too old to change. I don't have the strength or energy to change. This is just who I am and the way things will always be."

But this self-fulfilling message does not reflect the truth of what God says: "Forget the former things; do not dwell on the past. See, I am doing a new thing!" (Isaiah 43:18–19).

It's never too late to experience change in your life when you rely on God. You can partner with him in making the changes he wants you to experience by making different decisions. Based on his Word and wisdom gained from your experience, and led by the Holy Spirit and supported by some key trustworthy people in your life, you can go in a different direction. You can break default systems that feel ingrained and hardwired.

When you pre-decide how you will face future temptations based on the truth of who God says you are and the goodness of who he is, you align with his will. But this process of change is a collaborative effort: "Commit to the LORD whatever you do, and he will establish your plans" (Proverbs 16:3). When you decide now what you will do later, with God's help, you will determine your course of action before the moment of decision.

- How often do you catch yourself falling into the "I can't change" trap? How do you usually feel when this false message pops up in your mind?

- Do you usually consider yourself someone who is quick and confident in making decisions or someone who needs time and deliberation to think through all possible outcomes? How has this style of decision-making worked for you?

- How has God revealed to you that he wants to help you change the way you make decisions? How have you experienced his help in this endeavor already?

- What do you need to surrender to God in order to move the line and pre-decide how you will avoid and resist temptations?

CHOOSING HOW YOU CHOOSE

As you've likely experienced, pre-deciding that right thing to do would be easy enough if unpredictable variables didn't get thrown into the mix. In particular, we struggle when we're so tired of making decisions—usually called "decision fatigue"—that we would rather just give in without considering what we're doing and what the consequences will be.

Let's say you're trying to eat healthier and feel better in your body. You especially want to avoid too much sugar and caffeine, along with artificial ingredients that often hurt your body. Setting this goal, you know you should pack a healthy lunch at home to take with you for your day, but you're always so rushed to get out the door, you rarely pre-decide.

When you don't bring your lunch, you can either eat out, have something delivered, or snack on what's available. You don't have time to stop working to go out to eat, and it's too expensive to do so every day. So you default to what's available . . . chips and a soda from the office vending machines. Without pre-deciding a specific healthy lunch strategy, you set yourself up to cross the line.

There's also the fear of making a bad choice and suffering the consequences. The barbeque plate at the café down the block sounded like a good splurge until you realized you spent ten bucks in order to have heartburn the rest of the day. Plus, you didn't realize the ingredients in the special sauce must have included the very items you're trying to avoid—ones that upset your stomach.

Unexpected curveballs also wreak havoc with both your appetite and your options. When your boss wants a same-day turnaround on a big report, when you discover a coworker's been gossiping about you, when you spill coffee in your lap, your emotions respond accordingly. Resentment, betrayal, and frustration leave you feeling angry, hurt, and annoyed. You deserve something to help you feel better—maybe one of those donuts in the break room? Okay, because it's been such a tough day, maybe two.

Identifying the impact these three variables usually have on your daily decisions can help you rethink what you need to pre-decide. So for each category—decision fatigue, decision FOBI (fear of blowing it), and decision disrupters—answer the following questions as you assess each one's ability to hijack good decisions and push you closer toward the line.

DECISION FATIGUE: TOO MANY CHOICES, TOO MANY OPTIONS

- Which daily or regular decisions do you get tired of making? Why do you think they tend to drain your energy?

- When do you recently recall feeling overwhelmed by having to make a mundane decision? What contributed to your feeling overwhelmed prior to that moment?

- When have you avoided making a positive change—such as starting a workout program—because you dreaded the decisions involved?

DECISION FOBI (FEAR OF BLOWING IT): TOO MANY WORST CASES, TOO MANY UNCERTAIN OUTCOMES

- When making regular daily decisions, do you tend to stick with what you know works? Or do you like to try new options and enjoy some variety?

- When do you recall avoiding a decision because you were afraid you might make the wrong choice? Assuming you might make a wrong choice, what did you assume to be the consequences?

- Based on your history of making choices, what's your expectation bias? Do you assume you will usually experience positive results, or do you tend to jump to worst-case scenarios?

DECISION DISRUPTORS: TOO MANY CURVEBALLS, TOO MANY EMOTIONS

- Would your family and friends describe you as usually calm and steady or, more often, passionate and unpredictable?

- What role do you allow emotions to play in the decisions you make on a daily basis? Do you tend to base even mundane decisions—what to wear, what to eat—on logic and reason or on feelings and moods?

- What pushes your buttons and causes you to feel overwhelmed by a surge of emotions? When have you made a bad decision—or failed to decide at all—because your feelings got in the way?

DETERMINING YOUR DECISIONS

When you don't know exactly where the line falls, you don't recognize it until you've crossed it. "Oh, I guess I shouldn't have watched that movie with the romantic scenes in it. Even though there was nothing erotic or pornographic depicted, the situations still caused me to go to a certain place in my thoughts and imagination. A place where my decisions don't honor God or reflect who I want to be." With experiences such as this, you realize the line can easily become blurry. You thought you knew the border between black and white, right and wrong, tempting and sinful, only to discover a gray zone.

Or here's another example. If you battle alcoholism, you probably know it's not a good idea to work as a bartender or cashier in a liquor store. Why expose yourself to such blatant temptation, right? But finding the line that provides a safety buffer between you and what you're pre-deciding to avoid may be harder to discover. You might not realize the culture in a particular workplace until you're thrown into its midst. Suddenly, your boss throws a cocktail party, or your business hosts a wine-and-cheese event for a new client. Again, black and white seemed clear at first until you're thrust into a gray situation.

So based on what you read in chapters 1.1 through 1.3 in *Think Ahead*, as well as your responses so far in this first workbook session, let's practice identifying some of the lines you need to move. For example, if you want to avoid staying up too late and not getting enough sleep, you might identify the line as going to bed at 10 PM. But as you consider why this doesn't always work, you decide to move the line and stop watching Netflix an hour before bed, using that hour as a time to relax by reading or listening to calming music. Okay, now it's your turn:

Temptations to avoid	Where the line has been	Where to move the line
1.		
2.		
3.		
4.		
5.		

PLAN YOUR ESCAPE AND KNOW YOUR WEAK SPOT

When you get into a situation and suddenly everything gets dark, God promises to light up his exit for you, your sign to safety. To live a life of pre-decision, we learn to look for his signs before the lights go out.[4]

CRAIG GROESCHEL

If you fly often enough, you eventually get used to the preflight safety presentations required before takeoff. You know, the spiel about what to do in the unlikely event of an emergency, including how to maintain the flow of oxygen so you can keep breathing. While no one likes to think about the possibility of crashing when they fly, knowing what to do in the event of such an emergency can save your life. In particular, knowing the location of the nearest exit row greatly enhances your odds of survival.

In a recent study by Professor Ed Galea of the University of Greenwich, results revealed "that sitting within five rows of an emergency exit will drastically improve your chance of survival."[5] Galea studied configurations of the seating charts from more than 100 plane crashes. He also interviewed nearly 2,000 surviving passengers and more than 150 crew members aboard those flights. Based on both analytics and interviews, Galea concluded that the majority of survivors only had to move within five rows of their assigned seat in order to reach an exit row and escape. More than five rows and the likelihood of survival dropped.[6]

Similar studies have shown that knowing your nearest exit in public spaces, particularly the location of stairs and fire escapes, also saves lives. Obviously, locating a route of escape requires paying attention and knowing your own location in relation to what's around you. If you have physical limitations, you must also factor those into your exit strategy.

The same is true for escaping the magnetic pull of temptation. You need a predetermined plan for how to avoid crossing the line into sinful behavior. And in order to have an effective plan, you must know your weaknesses and limitations.

- How often do you fly in your current season of life? How closely do you pay attention to the preflight safety instructions?

- When you fly, do you usually make a mental note of the exit row nearest your assigned seat? How often do you locate the nearest exit when you're in a church, theater, or other public venue?

- Do you usually consider worst-case scenarios and plan how you would respond? Or are you more inclined to hope for the best and take your chances?

- When you think about the areas where you struggle with making good choices, what kinds of escape routes have you used in the past? How effective were they?

EXPLORING GOD'S WORD

You've likely recognized the passive-aggressive approach employed by the enemy when he is tempting you. Before you give in, the devil assures you that it's not a big deal, that everybody does it, that you're the only one you can count on to meet your needs. After you give in, he's the first accuser eager to shame you and magnify the impact and consequences of what you've done. Overall, the enemy likes to feed you lies about who you really are (an overcomer through the power of Jesus) and who God is (your loving Father) and the gift inside you (the Holy Spirit).

All the more reason to focus on what God says is true.

And what God's Word tells us is that we can overcome the enemy in the moment of temptation. Practically speaking, we can use our awareness of our weaknesses to move the line and protect ourselves. We can plan ahead and predetermine an escape plan to avoid being hijacked by temptation. In the collected wisdom of Solomon, we see a clear contrast: "A prudent person foresees danger and takes precautions. The simpleton goes blindly on and suffers the consequences" (Proverbs 27:12 NLT).

You're not a simpleton, or you wouldn't be reading this and trying to change. You're ready to change how you approach areas that typically ensnare you and pull you over the line. You're preparing before you're in trouble so you can be ready to stand firm in your faith. Which means it's time to get serious about wearing spiritual armor and planning your escape.

[11] Put on the full armor of God, so that you can take your stand against the devil's schemes. [12] For our struggle is not against flesh and blood, but against the rulers, against the authorities, against the powers of this dark world and against the spiritual forces of evil in the heavenly realms.

[13] Therefore put on the full armor of God, so that when the day of evil comes, you may be able to stand your ground, and after you have done everything, to stand. [14] Stand firm then, with the belt of truth buckled around your waist, with the breastplate of righteousness in place, [15] and with your feet fitted with the readiness that comes from the gospel of peace. [16] In addition to all this, take up the shield of faith, with which you can extinguish all the flaming arrows of the evil one. [17] Take the helmet of salvation and the sword of the Spirit, which is the word of God.

EPHESIANS 6:11–17

- Whether you're familiar with this passage or it's relatively new to you, what comes to mind when you think of putting on "the full armor of God" in order to resist "the devil's schemes"?

- Which defensive item stands out to you here? Why do you suppose you might especially need it right now?

- As you consider how to prepare for when you will be tempted in ways that target your weaknesses, how do you stand firm according to this passage?

- How does your faith provide a shield for anything the devil can throw at you? How does the sword of the Spirit cut through the lies, deception, and accusations of the enemy?

EMBRACING THE TRUTH

Sometimes it's challenging to know how a metaphor applies to you and your life in practical ways. Putting on the full armor of God may fit this category and cause you to wonder what it looks like for you. Perhaps the place to begin is simply recognizing the purpose of armor as a way to protect your vulnerable areas.

For centuries, warriors have used protective garments and defensive weapons to survive in battle. These specialized tactical pieces were often made of metal, wood, and stone—whatever was available and able to withstand blows from combat. While soldiers donned entire suits made of chain mail or forged iron by the Middle Ages, such comprehensive armor also limited mobility. Instead, many stuck with the tried and true—gear designed specifically for the most vulnerable body parts, such as the head, chest, groin, and feet.

This is the strategy implied in Ephesians. The belt of truth keeps you grounded and protected from the lies of the enemy—false assertions designed to throw you off-balance and harm your most vulnerable parts. Metal breastplates typically covered the pecs and chest to protect the heart and prevent penetration from a sword, dagger, knife, or club. The breastplate of righteousness then reminds us that our salvation has been secured by what Jesus did on the cross—not by our own efforts or ongoing merits. Rather than heavy boots, the gospel of peace provides an unshakable foundation of supernatural security that ensures you're ready for any and all circumstances.

The shield of faith blocks the direct assaults from the enemy while the helmet of salvation guards your mind with the assurance of God's unconditional love and grace. The sword of the Spirit, identified as God's Word, slices through illusions, delusions, deceptions, and darkness. Putting on all these pieces ensures you're prepared to resist injury and ready for any battle you may face, allowing you to "be strong in the Lord and in his mighty power" (Ephesians 6:10).

- How often do you prepare to resist the devil's schemes by utilizing the spiritual armor and weaponry available to you? What do you risk if you wait until you're in the midst of temptation or spiritual warfare before using this armor?

- Would you agree that basically all of these pieces of spiritual armor are forged by the truth of God's Word? How does immersing yourself consistently in his Word keep your armor intact?

- Which specific areas of your life seem most vulnerable to you right now? How can you utilize the armor of God to protect yourself and to avoid and resist temptation?

- How does relying on this supernatural armor prevent you from thinking you're strong enough on your own to overcome temptation? How does it help you pre-decide what you need in order to remain victorious over sin?

CHOOSING HOW YOU CHOOSE

Even if you understand how the armor of God can keep you ready for winning the battle over temptation, you might still wonder how to personalize it. You might assume that putting on spiritual armor amounts to doing what you already know or have been told to do—pray daily, study the Bible, meditate on God's truth, follow the example set by Jesus. While these spiritual practices do reinforce your armor, you can still personalize how you protect your most vulnerable areas and points of weakness.

Rather than simply repeating what you've been doing, what if you linked your spiritual disciplines with the weaknesses you're protecting? For example, let's say you want to limit the amount of time you spend on social media, knowing how it often causes you to waste time comparing yourself to others, feeling isolated, and making you feel as if you're missing out on all the great things everyone else on Instagram and TikTok seem to be doing. Perhaps you're unable to unplug completely from social media because you need access for work and like to stay connected to family and friends in distant places.

So perhaps tailoring a belt of truth to your personal needs involves noticing the triggers that lead you to compare and come up feeling insecure and less-than. Identifying these catalysts for comparison might allow you to avoid some of them altogether. And instead of continuing to scroll and drool over your friend's beautiful family and their latest vacation, maybe you hit pause and realize how this triggers envy and insecurity in you. As soon as you realize the possibility for comparison, you can focus instead on who you are in Christ—a beloved child of God, a forgiven co-heir with Jesus, a temple for the Holy Spirit, an overcomer.

Rather than simply assuming you're putting on a "one size fits all" belt of truth, you cinch it to the truth you need most to keep you grounded and protected. Now that you've got the idea, go through these pieces of armor and specify how you can customize them, using them to help you pre-decide strategies, protect your weaknesses, and escape from sin by avoiding temptations.

Item of armor	Purpose	Customized for you
Belt of Truth		
Breastplate of Righteousness		
Gospel of Peace		
Shield of Faith		
Helmet of Salvation		
Sword of the Spirit		

DETERMINING YOUR DECISIONS

When tempted in the heat of the moment, we often feel like we have no choice, like we don't have enough strength, energy, or willpower to resist the allure of what's before us. Whether it's looking at certain images online, hitting the PayPal button on a favorite retail site, opening the container of chocolate gelato before bedtime, or visiting the new craft brewery that just opened, we can't wait until those opportunities are right in front of us.

Before we expose ourselves to potential temptation, we must remember these words from Paul:

> God is faithful, so He will not allow you to be tempted beyond what you are able, but with the temptation will provide the way of escape also, so that you will be able to endure it.
>
> 1 CORINTHIANS 10:13 NASB

Knowing God provides a way of escape from every temptation, we can think ahead and plan how to dodge the pull we feel once we're tempted. With this strategy in mind, we can protect ourselves in areas where we're particularly vulnerable.

Reread chapter 1.6 in *Think Ahead* and then review your answers for the questions at the end of part 1 on page 67. If you dodged being honest about what you know causes you to struggle, then now is the time to come clean. Consider ways you can not only move the line but avoid it altogether. That might mean choosing not to be alone in certain situations. Or taking a different route home from work. Or not traveling away from home overnight without safeguards such as having your spouse or a trusted friend accompany you.

Honesty is imperative, though, for your escape plan to work. No one else needs to see your answers unless you decide to share them with others you trust for purposes of support and accountability. Which, in fact, is one of the most powerful ways to plan your escape route—with the help of others. Bringing your struggles into the light and acknowledging them takes away so much of their power. Plus, you enlist others who can check on you, encourage you, and pray for you.

So think about the temptations that hold the most appeal for you, and then come up with at least one feasible plan of escape the next time you are aware that it's near.

Temptation	My weakness it targets	My escape plan
1.		
2.		
3.		
4.		
5.		

PART 2

I WILL BE DEVOTED

When trying to pre-decide how you will handle certain situations and make better decisions, your success relies on your foundational basis. In other words, your ultimate priorities determine how you go about deciding. You may say you're devoted to God, but if he is not anchoring every area of your life, then your choices will reveal this discrepancy. By pre-deciding that you will be devoted, you put God first in all areas of your life, eliminating distractions and implementing a lifestyle centered on your relationship with him. Here are the key principles you will learn in part 2:

- We can't be part-time followers of Christ. We must think ahead and pre-decide to be devoted to pursuing Jesus.
- When you understand who God is and what he's done for you, nothing else makes sense but to put him first.
- Devotion is reflected by putting God first in your thoughts, your money, your decisions, your time, and what you care about.
- The devil doesn't need to destroy you if he can divide your mind, discourage your faith, and distract you from what matters most.
- Prioritizing your devotion to Jesus requires minimizing distractions and eliminating things—sometimes good things—from your life.
- To spend undistracted time with Jesus, pre-decide and prioritize an intentional strategy—a rule of life—that includes a time, a place, and a plan.

WHAT A DEVOTED LIFE LOOKS (AND DOESN'T LOOK) LIKE

If you don't put God first, you'll put something else first, and nothing else can handle the pressure of being the most important thing in your life.[7]

CRAIG GROESCHEL

Parents usually encourage their kids to participate in sports, hoping they will enjoy the camaraderie and benefit from the discipline. Some moms and dads can become a bit obsessive about pushing their sons and daughters to not only participate but to be the best. Most sports parents, though, don't come close to the devotion Richard Williams invested in the tennis careers of his daughters, Venus and Serena.

Williams's intense focus was depicted in the Academy Award-winning film *King Richard*, revealing how his dream determined his family's priorities based on what would best develop the athletic potential of his girls. Despite working nights as a security guard, Williams encouraged his young daughters to have fun and do their best on the crumbling tennis courts of Compton, a crime-ridden area of southern Los Angeles, where they lived at the time. Within a few short years, Williams had moved his family to Florida for a couple of reasons—warm weather conducive to playing year-round and some of the finest tennis coaches in the world.[8]

Decades later, the fruits of his relentless drive are more than evident. The names Venus and Serena have become synonymous with their iconic successful careers. Venus set a high standard for success with seven Grand Slam singles titles, five Wimbledon championships, and four Olympic gold medals. Serena managed to exceed that feat with twenty-three Grand Slam singles championships, seven Wimbledon titles, and four Olympic gold medals of her own.

Despite their amazing success, the cost of their father's dream cannot be calculated. "The size and scope of the dream was so huge that it bordered on insanity," observed actor Will Smith, whose portrayal of Williams won an Oscar. "It's sort of where you have to live if you want to do something that's never been done before."[9]

- What's your take on parents like Richard Williams who are so driven in pursuit of fulfilling the dream they have for their children? Can you relate?

- Based on how you spend your time, attention, energy, and money, what are the priorities of your family right now?

- When have you been driven to attain a goal or fulfill a pursuit at virtually any cost? How would you describe the process required for reaching your achievement?

- When you think about devoting your life to a singular focus, what comes to mind? How does this manifest in your life presently?

EXPLORING GOD'S WORD

Whatever you value tends to influence the way you make decisions.

If you're focused on advancing in your career, then your choices—everything from how you dress to what you talk about to where you live—likely reflect your professional aspirations. If looking your best so that others find you attractive takes center stage, then what you eat, how you exercise, and who you follow on social media gets decided based on prioritizing your image. It might be accumulating enough money to retire early or simply paying off old loans and getting out of debt. Based on how much time you spend thinking about it, how much money you spend, and how much your attention revolves around it, your decisions will flow in the same direction.

God wants to be central in your life. He longs for your relationship with him to be what matters most to you. He can guide, direct, and empower you to make decisions that honor him and fulfill you—if you put him first. Jesus emphasized this truth when telling his followers:

[19] "Do not store up for yourselves treasures on earth, where moths and vermin destroy, and where thieves break in and steal. [20] But store up for yourselves treasures in heaven, where moths and vermin do not destroy,

and where thieves do not break in and steal. [21] For where your treasure is, there your heart will be also."

MATTHEW 6:19–21

We tend to think of money as our primary treasure here on earth. But really, anything that consumes your thoughts, time, and attention reflects what you treasure as well. In other words, your earthly treasures are whatever you prize most. When you value heavenly treasures more, however, you invest in a legacy that lasts longer than anything contained in a bank account, spacious home, or jewelry box. Your heart focuses on what you treasure, and what you treasure consumes your heart.

- When have you realized the limitations of focusing on earthly treasures? When have you lost something material that mattered greatly to you?

- What are some things you treasure in this life besides money or wealth? How have these treasures required your attention and determined how you've made certain decisions?

- Think back on what's been most important to you over the past week. What decisions did you make that reflect its importance to you?

- How have you pursued heavenly treasures in the past? How did their value to you influence the decisions you made?

EMBRACING THE TRUTH

Whatever we're devoted to pursuing usually fills up our lives. Whether it's advancing in our career, raising a healthy family, moving to a nicer home, or running a marathon, we hone in on things that contribute to attaining this goal and let go of other things. We make more room in our lives for our devotion to these goals, sacrificing whatever—and often whoever—doesn't help us advance. Depending on what we're moving toward, however, we may lose our sense of direction.

When we devote ourselves to knowing, loving, and serving God, we discover the cost. We may not advance at work because we're not willing to idolize a promotion. We may discover that our family can be healthy without it looking the way we thought it had to look. We may need to stay where we are and trust God for when or if we move to another home. We may have to extend our training and go more slowly in preparing for a marathon as we put running in balance with other priorities. Otherwise, we allow something other than God to control our lives and make our decisions.

Jesus addressed this problem in a parable he told his followers:

[16] "The ground of a certain rich man yielded an abundant harvest. [17] He thought to himself, 'What shall I do? I have no place to store my crops.'

[18] "Then he said, 'This is what I'll do. I will tear down my barns and build bigger ones, and there I will store my surplus grain. [19] And I'll say to myself, "You have plenty of grain laid up for many years. Take life easy; eat, drink and be merry."'

[20] "But God said to him, 'You fool! This very night your life will be demanded from you. Then who will get what you have prepared for yourself?'

[21] "This is how it will be with whoever stores up things for themselves but is not rich toward God."

LUKE 12:16–21

● What word or phrase jumps out at you? Why do you suppose it resonates?

- When have you pursued bigger barns to accommodate your priority rather than focused on God as the center of your life?

- What are you most tempted to store up or accumulate in your life? Money, possessions, status symbols—or awards, achievements, attention?

- When have you realized you were putting something in your life ahead of God? What did you have to surrender in order to restore your devotion to him?

CHOOSING HOW YOU CHOOSE

You may be struggling to admit that you put anything before God. In completing this study, however, you're indicating a desire to grow closer to him and to base your decisions on what pleases him. Therefore, before you go any further in considering what influences the way you make decisions, you need to come clean.

If you want to be a full-time follower of Jesus, then recognizing that you're currently part-time is the place to start. Even if you're following him all the time every day, you probably have areas in your life that are harder to surrender than others. Which is why you want help thinking ahead and making better decisions—to align what you believe with how you live your life.

In order to make God your top priority, it also helps to remain vigilant about the things that tend to encroach on your life. Perennial busyness affects virtually everyone, but as you've likely realized by now, you spend your precious commodity of time on what you care most about. If not, then you're wasting your most limited resource in this life. Similarly with your finances and material resources. It may disrupt you to admit it, but your lifestyle—right now at this moment—reveals a good deal of what you value most. If you're serious about being devoted to God, and using your divine devotion as a chisel for how you carve out your life, then it's worth taking another look at your inventory of priorities.

Toward this goal, review your responses to the exercises at the end of part 2 in *Think Ahead*, particularly the ones related to the five signs indicating your devotion to God. Based on your responses, take this opportunity to dive deeper and consider how to shift all five in alignment with your heart's deepest devotion.

THOUGHTS

- Considering all you juggle on a typical day, what topics, problems, issues, struggles, and relationships occupy the most real estate in your mind? List them below, and be as specific as possible.

Topics (about work, home, school, church, community):

Problems (related to work, money, family, your responsibilities, or others):

Issues (personal struggles and secrets, job concerns, worries about others):

Struggles (conflicts with yourself and with others, with making changes):

Relationships (with spouse, children, parents, coworkers, neighbors):

- What else usually occupies your thoughts?

FINANCES

- Knowing your heart's concerns are reflected in where your money goes, what do you see when you review your budget, your bank statements, your credit card usage, your savings, and, of course, what you give to God?

- What surprises you most about where your money is going right now? Why?

- What keeps you from using your money to show your devotion to God? How can you realign this imbalance?

DECISIONS

- What are the biggest decisions with which you're currently wrestling? How have you pursued God's will in making these decisions?

- What decisions have you been postponing for too long? What have you been waiting on?

- How often do you pray about making these decisions, or decisions in general, before choosing a direction and taking action?

TIME

- If you review your schedule or calendar for the past week, what does it appear you value most?

- What time-consumers can be reduced or eliminated in order for you to spend more time with God?

- Ideally, how would you spend your time on an average day? How would this allocation reflect your devotion to God?

HEARTBREAK

- What issues, individuals, and struggles stir your heart most often? What have you sensed God calling you to do regarding these areas?

- When have you been able to reflect your devotion to God in helping another person deal with their loss, struggle, or heartbreak?

- How often do you compartmentalize your feelings so that they do not interfere with your daily functions? What might you discover if you allow yourself to own and express them?

DETERMINING YOUR DECISIONS

You may feel like you have little control over certain aspects of these five key areas, but you probably have more power to change than you usually exercise. It's easy to do what others expect us to do to avoid upsetting them or rocking the boat. But sometimes you have to risk making changes in the way you live in order to grow closer to God—and make better decisions.

- Which of the five areas are you reluctant to adjust or change because of how others might react? Or how they might view you?

- When have you recently avoided telling the truth in love to someone and allowed them to command more of you and your resources than is healthy?

Overlooked distractions can often be eliminated as well, though you may be uncomfortable getting rid of them at first. Sometimes we keep busy to avoid doing hard things or taking personal risks. Scrolling and browsing online becomes a habit to fill our time rather than a limited, intentional activity. Or maybe your default is binge-watching Netflix, going to the gym, gaming, or following sports. Not bad activities until you're allowing them to consume time unintentionally.

- Which default habits and time-wasters need to be dialed down or eliminated from your life?

- What have they been providing for you—comfort, escape from boredom, excitement, romance, something else?

Finally, you may be facing some barriers to your relationship with God that you have avoided until now. It might be a habit or addiction that requires you to ask for help—from God and from others. It could be wounds from your past that you've tried to ignore but continue to disrupt your thoughts and feelings. You might need to have a conversation with someone, ask for their forgiveness, or resolve a lingering conflict. Whatever this barrier might be, you know it's getting in the way of your devotion to God.

- What burdens have you been carrying that consume too much of your thoughts, energy, and attention?

- What's one step you can take today in order to begin moving through them, resolving them, or getting help with them?

CONNECTION, DISTRACTION, AND A GAME PLAN

Full devotion to God will never happen by accident.
That's why we have to pre-decide: I am going to seek God first.[10]

CRAIG GROESCHEL

US Surgeon General Dr. Vivek Murthy recently launched a major initiative to address our country's "epidemic of loneliness and isolation."[11] This campaign draws from similar ones in other countries, particularly Japan and the United Kingdom, which respectively include a government position known as the Minister of Loneliness. These leaders were strategizing how to overcome the serious health effects years before the COVID pandemic, which only increased the isolation and social separation due to the necessity of quarantines.[12]

Dr. Murthy, along with the British Minister of Loneliness, Baroness Diana Barran, have cited direct links between loneliness and many life-threatening diseases and illnesses, including heart disease, stroke, diabetes, dementia, anxiety and depression, and suicide. In the United States, estimates of those suffering run as high as nearly half the population, or more than 150 million people. Global experts stress that the primary remedy is forming strong connections and ongoing relationships within a supportive community. In a press conference Dr. Murthy stated, "Social connection is as essential to humanity as food, water or shelter."[13]

One obvious irony in acknowledging the damage done by social isolation and loneliness stems from the connectivity afforded by technology. Thanks to the internet and social media, one person can literally communicate with millions of other individuals around the world. Unfortunately, that same ability to connect online seems to have contributed to the global epidemic of loneliness. The impact of loneliness certainly isn't caused by our ability to relate online, but most experts agree it has been a factor.

Communicating and connecting online is simply not an adequate substitute for in-person conversations, affectionate touch, and shared experiences. Government leaders and medical experts agree that overcoming loneliness requires being intentional about making and sustaining relationships. It requires being aware of the problem and making a strategic plan for lifesaving connection.

- How aware are you of the impact of loneliness and isolation on people around the world currently? How have you witnessed its impact in your community?

- Does the direct link between loneliness and serious health risks surprise you? Why do you suppose isolation and loneliness compound factors leading to disease and mental illness?

- How often do you battle feeling lonely and isolated in your life? What impact has this had on your health?

- What do you suppose is the impact of loneliness and isolation on one's relationship with God? Why?

EXPLORING GOD'S WORD

The global loneliness epidemic reminds us that quality of relationships ultimately matters more than quantity. Perhaps this is why individuals can have hundreds or thousands of social media friends and followers while being isolated from the benefits of in-person relationships. In order for a relationship to have a positive impact, the connection requires ongoing attention. Too often, it's easy to get so caught up in our busy lives that we overlook our own emotional need for connection as well as that of others.

The same is true for your relationship with God. Unless you pre-decide to be intentional about your devotion to knowing him, you can remain a part-time follower. You can remain busy and pulled in numerous directions by relentless responsibilities and urgent demands. You can say a prayer at mealtime or on the fly. You can go to church once a week or when you can fit it in. Growing deeper in your faith and closer to God will never happen this way, though.

Similar to human relationships, our devoted relationship with God requires establishing connection, eliminating distractions, and following an intentional strategy. We see this in Jesus' visit with his friends Mary and Martha. While these sisters hosted Jesus in their home, each seemed to have a different priority. Read what Jesus had to say about their choices and answer the questions that follow:

[38] As Jesus and his disciples were on their way, he came to a village where a woman named Martha opened her home to him. [39] She had a sister called Mary, who sat at the Lord's feet listening to what he said. [40] But Martha was distracted by all the preparations that had to be made. She came to him and asked, "Lord, don't you care that my sister has left me to do the work by myself? Tell her to help me!"

[41] "Martha, Martha," the Lord answered, "you are worried and upset about many things, [42] but few things are needed—or indeed only one. Mary has chosen what is better, and it will not be taken away from her."

LUKE 10:38–42

- Based on what Jesus said, how should Martha have regarded all the preparations that had to be made? Can you relate to Martha's dilemma in this situation?

- What stirs inside you when hearing Jesus speak these words directly to you: "You are worried and upset about many things, but few things are needed—or indeed only one"?

- Out of the "many things" that cause you to be worried and upset, which are the "few things" needed? What is your "only one"?

- How well have you balanced Martha's concern about preparations with Mary's focus on Jesus? What is your takeaway from their encounter with the Lord?

EMBRACING THE TRUTH

When you pre-decide to devote yourself to God, you are also choosing to eliminate distractions and to make a game plan. Jesus said, "No one can serve two masters. Either you will hate the one and love the other, or you will be devoted to the one and despise the other. You cannot serve both God and money" (Matthew 6:24). Based on God's desire to be first in your life, it's clear you cannot serve both God and anything else. Our Creator knows that we are made in his image and designed for spiritual intimacy with him.

In order to experience this intimacy for which you're made, you must make knowing and experiencing God your priority. While you may have considered what this commitment required when you first became a follower of Jesus, you also have to continue counting the cost and paying the price throughout your life. Basically, this decision requires agreeing to pay the price regardless of how you feel or how your circumstances change. Jesus illustrated this process with two comparisons:

> [28] "Suppose one of you wants to build a tower. Won't you first sit down and estimate the cost to see if you have enough money to complete it? [29] For if you lay the foundation and are not able to finish it, everyone who sees it will ridicule you, [30] saying, 'This person began to build and wasn't able to finish.'
>
> [31] "Or suppose a king is about to go to war against another king. Won't he first sit down and consider whether he is able with ten thousand men to oppose the one coming against him with twenty thousand? [32] If he is not able, he will send a delegation while the other is still a long way off and will ask for terms of peace. [33] In the same way, those of you who do not give up everything you have cannot be my disciples."
>
> LUKE 14:28–33

- When you became a believer, what did it mean for you to count the cost of following Jesus? What changes did you make in how you lived your life?

- What specifically have you given up in order to make Christ your top priority? What are you still in the process of giving up?

- Which of these two illustrations, building a tower or going to war, resonates with you most? Why?

- Which relationships and unexpected events have seemed to increase the cost of your commitment to God? How have they made it harder for you to prioritize your relationship with Jesus?

CHOOSING HOW YOU CHOOSE

There's no doubt about it: God asks a lot of you—*everything*, in fact. When you're pre-deciding to be devoted to him and your relationship with him, you might feel a little ambivalent or even resentful at times. You start focusing on what you're giving up and what you apparently aren't allowed to enjoy in order to obey God and follow Christ's example. In the midst of painful circumstances and devastating losses, you may lose sight of God's promises, stop trusting in his Word, and start to doubt your devotion.

Those valleys are to be expected on your journey of faith. Which is why it's important to pre-decide that your commitment to God is about more than just your mountaintop experiences. It's about remembering how much he loves you and all he has done for you. God asks you to put him first because he has already put you first: "We love because he first loved us" (1 John 4:19).

Even before you were born, God loved you and had pre-decided to make the ultimate sacrifice—the death of his Son, Jesus, on the cross—so you could experience his love: "Even before he made the world, God loved us and chose us in Christ to be holy and without fault in his eyes. God decided in advance to adopt us into his own family by bringing us to himself through Jesus Christ. This is what he wanted to do, and it gave him great pleasure" (Ephesians 1:4–5 NLT).

That's how much you matter to God.

That's how much he loves you.

Your response to such unconditional, limitless love requires holding nothing back and letting nothing come between you and God. Toward this goal, you will likely find it helpful to develop a "rule of life," a kind of mission statement for your faith and how you live it out. After reviewing chapter 2.5 in *Think Ahead*, write out a rule of life reflecting your pre-decision to remain devoted to God. Think of this rule of life as a draft, a work in progress that you can revise as you grow in your faith. Using the prompts below, include two key components, an overall statement of your devotion to God along with some smaller rules to support your rule of life.

MY RULE OF LIFE

I am devoted to God because _____ and want to show my devotion by being more focused on _____ _____ and less focused on _____ _____ _____ .

To help me remain focused on God as my life's priority, I will use the following rules and practices:

1.

2.

3.

4.

5.

DETERMINING YOUR DECISIONS

When something is important to you, you plan it out ahead of time. When someone is important to you, you plan to make spending time together a priority. At first it might seem like you enjoy being with them so much that you don't need a plan. But over time, as your life gets busy and other demands vie for your attention, you realize that in order to grow in your relationship, you need to plan ahead.

For example, you might plan a weekly date night with your spouse or have a regular time to meet your best friend for coffee at a specific café. You might take your kids to the climbing wall every Saturday to ensure your time together. You've learned that if you don't have a plan—one that includes a place, a time, and an activity or shared experience—then something else always interferes and prevents you from connecting consistently.

When you pre-decide to be devoted to God, you honor your commitment by making a plan for when, where, and how you will spend quality time together. Rather than just squeezing in a prayer when you think of him or skimming a devotional over breakfast, you make a plan to slow down and focus on the relationship that means the most to you. Sure, you will need to be flexible and include variety and spontaneity, just as you would for any relationship. But practicing your devotion means pre-deciding that there must be a plan.

Use the following questions to help you think about how you usually spend time with God and how you would like to plan moving forward.

- On a scale of 1 to 10, with 1 being inconsistent and 10 being perfectly consistent, how would you rate your current plan for spending time with God? Why?

- What's usually been the problem in spending quality time with the Lord—finding and making the time, choosing a place without interruptions, or knowing what to do? Something else?

- What's worked well for you in the past when spending time with God? Where do you enjoy focusing on him the most?

- What kinds of activities facilitate your ability to connect with and experience God? Check all that apply:

  ❏ Devotionals (List a favorite here: _____)
  ❏ Bible study (What method of study do you prefer?)
  ❏ Praise and worship music (Your go-to playlist includes: _____
  _____)
  ❏ Prayer time (What categories do you usually use when praying?)
  ❏ Serving others (What acts of service draw you closer to God?)
  ❏ Creative expression (What do you like to draw, write, make?)

- Based on your response, what plan do you want to make moving forward?

Time:
Place:
Activity/experience:

PART 3

I WILL BE FAITHFUL

When you are devoted and make God your priority, then faithfulness follows. You want to honor him in everything you do, and your decisions reflect your consistent willingness to trust him. You have pre-decided that your obedience grows out of the depth of your relationship with Jesus as you follow the example he set for how to interact with others. Being faithful means not only focusing your time and attention on God but also stewarding all resources entrusted to you. Your faithfulness allows you to practice generosity, compassion, and hospitality for God's glory and the advancement of his kingdom. Here are the key principles you will learn in part 3:

- You must pre-decide to be faithful because it will never happen by accident.
- Every interaction is an opportunity to add value, every resource an opportunity to multiply, and every prompting an opportunity to obey God.
- Rather than living a natural, self-focused life, you can live a supernatural, others-focused life because the Holy Spirit lives in you.
- Multiplying what you've been given in the kingdom of God is faithfulness.
- Because God is relational, he loves to speak to us through his Word and his Spirit, through circumstances, and through other people.
- When God prompts, directs, or speaks to you, your response will take faith.
- You will overestimate what you can do in the short run but vastly underestimate what God can do through a lifetime of faithfulness.
- When you're faithful with a little, God will trust you with much.

EVERY INTERACTION IS AN OPPORTUNITY TO ADD VALUE

When we choose to be faithful, we have no idea how God might use even a single word of encouragement to change someone's life.[14]

CRAIG GROESCHEL

Joanna Gaines has become one of the most successful interior designers in the US in a relatively short period of time. Together with her husband, Chip, Joanna has been credited with the mainstream popularity of "farmhouse style," a hallmark feature in the homes they renovate. Much of Joanna's ability to transform an aging fixer-upper into a warm, inviting, contemporary home stems from her ability to imagine possibilities.[15]

"Doing flips that are fast and fun is how I fell in love with design in the first place," she revealed to *Architectural Digest*. "They're proof that you don't necessarily have to take down walls or have a huge budget to transform a space—sometimes even small adjustments can make a big impact."[16] Joanna clearly has a creative knack for knowing which interior elements to keep and which to alter or eliminate. She knows how to make interiors inviting by recognizing opportunities for adding functional value, which in turn adds market value.

Unlike Joanna Gaines and other talented designers, many people struggle to recognize the potential when they walk into a room. They overlook the ways that professionals with natural talent, educational training, and personal experience view architectural features and interior proportions. With practice and passion, however, would-be designers learn to see beyond what's in front of them.

When it comes to our interactions with other people, we can follow a similar example set by Jesus. He transformed human lives by knowing every encounter with someone contained an opportunity for blessing them.

- What do you usually notice when entering a home for the first time? What details tend to draw your attention?

- How often do you imagine ways a space could be more functional, inviting, and attractive? How often do you take steps to make such changes or help others make these changes?

- When you meet other people for the first time, do you tend to be more curious about them or more skeptical of them? Do you assume they want something from you or that you have something to offer them? Both?

- How would you interact differently with other people if you focused on looking for ways to add value to your encounter? Why?

EXPLORING GOD'S WORD

Jesus added value to every human interaction he had during his life on earth. He saw them beyond their appearance, their social status, their titles or wealth. He saw their hearts, their needs, their fears and worries. He offered himself to each person in a unique way that reflected the love of his Father. The example Jesus set inspires us to look for creative ways to engage others.

Take Zacchaeus, for example. You may not be able to imagine the encounter between Jesus and Zacchaeus without humming that song you learned as a child in Sunday school about Zac being such a "wee little man." Whether you learned that memorable tune or not, its lyrics remind us that Zacchaeus was used to being overlooked. Short in stature and apparently despised for his corrupt profession as a tax collector, Zacchaeus heard that the man claiming to be the Messiah would be passing through town (Luke 19:1–10). Too short to see above the gathering crowd, he ran ahead of Jesus and climbed a sycamore-fig tree.

Perhaps Zac thought no one would see him up there. That he could just remain invisible and spy on this visitor's interactions with the crowd. Which likely means that the diminutive tax man was surprised—if not startled—to look down and see Jesus looking up at him. "Zacchaeus, come down immediately. I must stay at your house today," Jesus said. So the wee little man "came down at once and welcomed him gladly" (Luke 19:5–6).

Their exchange did not go unnoticed, though. Onlookers immediately threw shade—and shame—on them both: "He has gone to be the guest of a sinner" (Luke 19:7). In one fell swoop, they condemned Zacchaeus as a sinner and implied Jesus must not be much better if he's willing to be the tax collector's guest. But as you can see below, Jesus had the last word, making it clear that his encounter with Zacchaeus wasn't an exception but the way he approached everyone he met.

[1] Jesus entered Jericho and was passing through. [2] A man was there by the name of Zacchaeus; he was a chief tax collector and was wealthy. [3] He wanted to see who Jesus was, but because he was short he could not see over the crowd. [4] So he ran ahead and climbed a sycamore-fig tree to see him, since Jesus was coming that way.

[5] When Jesus reached the spot, he looked up and said to him, "Zacchaeus, come down immediately. I must stay at your house today." [6] So he came down at once and welcomed him gladly.

[7] All the people saw this and began to mutter, "He has gone to be the guest of a sinner."

[8] But Zacchaeus stood up and said to the Lord, "Look, Lord! Here and now I give half of my possessions to the poor, and if I have cheated anybody out of anything, I will pay back four times the amount."

[9] Jesus said to him, "Today salvation has come to this house, because this man, too, is a son of Abraham. [10] For the Son of Man came to seek and to save the lost."

LUKE 19:1–10

- Have you ever been in a situation where you felt like Zacchaeus, wanting to blend into a crowd only to be singled out? If so, how would you describe it?

- What was uniquely unexpected about what Jesus said to Zacchaeus and the way he viewed the need of this man whom others despised?

- What implied message did Jesus convey by inviting himself to the tax collector's house for a meal? How did Zacchaeus respond to this underlying message?

- How does the way Jesus interacted with Zacchaeus inspire you to relate to people whom others condemn? Can you think of anyone in your life right now who's like Zacchaeus?

EMBRACING THE TRUTH

Just as he demonstrated with Zacchaeus, Jesus viewed every opportunity as a way to encourage, to meet a need, to share God's grace. He never followed popular opinion or let the criticism or contempt of others prevent him from conversing, healing, touching, or eating with someone Christ encountered. As his followers, we are called to follow his example and consider every interaction with another person as an opportunity to add value to their lives.

We do this by showing them grace—just as Jesus did with the woman caught in adultery and brought before him (John 8:10–11). We do this by meeting needs—just as Jesus did with the crowd of more than 5,000 who needed lunch (see Matthew 14:13–21). We do this by forgiving others when they hurt us or mess up—just as Jesus did when his friend and disciple Peter denied even knowing him (John 18 and John 21). We do this by building up others when they are suffering or grieving—just as Jesus did when his disciples began worrying about all the turmoil surrounding them (Matthew 6:31–34). We do this by blessing, serving, and speaking words of life—just as Jesus did by washing the feet of his disciples at their last meal together before his death (John 13:1–5).

If you are faithfully following Jesus, every interaction is an opportunity to add value.

- What stands out to you about the way Jesus engaged with everyone he met? How did he often surprise them or upend their expectations?

- How often do you think about Jesus' relational style when you're interacting with others? When has recalling the way Jesus added value to others caused you to be more patient, kind, compassionate, or forgiving?

- Based on what you know about your own relational style, what do you often do when interacting with others that reflects Christ's love? What do you often do, or fail to do, that needs to change in order to add value to your interactions?

- Of the many encounters Jesus had with individuals during his life on earth, which ones stand out to you? Why?

CHOOSING HOW YOU CHOOSE

Choosing to be faithful by adding value to others means pre-deciding to put them before yourself. Viewing every interaction you have—with difficult family members, inconsiderate neighbors, competitive coworkers, comparative friends, overwhelmed waitstaff, slow cashiers, everyone—as an opportunity to add value to their lives requires being intentional. It asks you to see people beyond the roles they play, the jobs they do, the contextual scripts. It requires seeing them the way Jesus saw them—vulnerable, needy, frustrated, hurting, lonely, ashamed, hungry, thirsty, prideful, humble, and more like us than different.

Pre-deciding to be faithful by adding value to others also demands that you suffer, that you wait, that you take time, that you give, that you listen, and that you love. These responses may not come naturally—in fact, they may often go against your human tendency to overlook others because you're so caught up in your own life. Which is why faithfulness must be intentional. You're never going to fall into faithfulness or automatically put others' needs before your own.

- What are some of the reasons that you sometimes struggle to add value to others when you interact? Check all that apply.

  ❑ Too busy, usually in a hurry
  ❑ Impatient, looking ahead
  ❑ Defensive, skeptical of others' motives
  ❑ Concerned it will require too much
  ❑ Fear of getting too involved in others' problems
  ❑ Kindness might be exploited
  ❑ Others talk too much
  ❑ Too many responsibilities and obligations already
  ❑ Can't afford possible financial expense
  ❑ Sets precedent for them to want more from me
  ❑ Makes me feel too vulnerable
  ❑ Other: _____

- Generally, when you're with the people you encounter daily, are you more inclined to be reserved and contained or outgoing and curious?

- What aspects of adding value to others makes you most uncomfortable? Why?

- When have you most recently let others see Jesus in you by the way you interacted with them?

DETERMINING YOUR DECISIONS

One of the most powerful motivators for being faithful and adding value when you interact with others is your own experience. You have undoubtedly been blessed, comforted, encouraged, supported, and inspired by the way so many others have chosen to interact with you. There are probably a few key people who were instrumental in leading you to follow Jesus. Others may have helped you grow, provided friendship and fellowship, offered wise counsel, or given you money or material items to meet your needs.

Reviewing chapter 3.2 in *Think Ahead*, you see the example that I cited as being pivotal in my life and in my calling. After being told that I was not cut out for the ministry, I was devastated and shaken—until my pastor and mentor Nick reminded me that no human being could stop me from doing what God had called me to do. With kindness and compassion, wisdom and understanding, Nick cut through the pain of my rejection and added inestimable value to someone he believed in and cared about.

You may have someone like Nick in your own life, someone who offered encouragement, support, or wisdom at a crucial turning point for you. These individuals show us what Jesus looks like in how we interact with others as well. They reinforce Christ's example, demonstrate generosity, and minimize the personal cost in order to make a crucial difference for others.

You have most likely already added value to the lives of the many people you've encountered in your life. But now is the time to be even more determined to show them what they likely don't expect—love and acceptance, patience and forgiveness, provision and encouragement. Show your faithfulness by surprising them with the grace of Jesus.

- Who comes to mind when you think about people who have added spiritual value to your life? Who are the two or three who have been there for you at crucial moments?

- Based on all you've received from them and the example set by Jesus, who in your life right now can you bless in a significant way?

EVERY RESOURCE AND PROMPTING IS AN OPPORTUNITY

If you commit to following Jesus, he will lead you.
He will prompt you. Faithfulness means feeling compelled to obey,
even when you don't know what will happen next. [17]

CRAIG GROESCHEL

You never know when a temporary prompting from God will become a permanent calling on your life. Just ask Dr. David Vanderpool. A dedicated and successful surgeon, Dr. Vanderpool and his wife, Laurie, enjoyed a fulfilling life in an affluent part of Nashville, Tennessee. They were active in their church and other ministries, supported many community programs, and raised their family with the same Christian values they held.

With experience as a medical missionary, Dr. Vanderpool felt called to help residents in Haiti following the devastating earthquake there in 2010. Registering

7.0 in magnitude with aftershocks of 5.9 and 5.5, the disaster claimed more than 300,000 lives, with an unknown number of wounded and injured.[18] In his book *Live Beyond*, Dr. Vanderpool explained, "I thought that I was just going to Haiti for a few weeks to provide disaster relief. Little did I know that weeks would turn into months, and three years later, Haiti would become my permanent home. Little did I know that when the Lord gripped me to go in 2010, it was a permanent grip."[19]

Their obedience to God's prompting in the wake of such overwhelming need prompted the Vanderpools to sell their home and all their belongings in order to move to Thomazeau, Haiti, and establish a medical clinic as well as a school. Today, LiveBeyond, as their medical ministry is called, has saved hundreds if not thousands of lives by offering free medical treatment, neonatal care for mothers, and weekly food distributions. They have multiplied their resources beyond measure as they continue to advance God's kingdom.

- Can you relate to what Dr. Vanderpool and his family experienced in response to God's prompting? What intrigues you most about their story?

- While the Vanderpools' choices may seem extreme, they did not decide to move to Haiti all at once. Where or in whom are you currently investing your resources and wish to invest more?

- Does the Vanderpools' story scare you, excite you, or both? Why?

- What's a need—either large or small, local or global—that you feel prompted to address in some way? What does this need stir in you?

EXPLORING GOD'S WORD

Your faithfulness to God is reflected by how you handle the resources he's entrusted to you. Everything you have comes from him so that you can fulfill your purpose in serving others and advancing his kingdom. Every talent, ability, skill, and experience along with every dollar, possession, vehicle, and gadget—God trusts you to use those for more than your own pleasure and convenience.

Faithfully stewarding what the Lord has given you is not about maintaining status quo either. God wants you taking risks to invest what he's given you to multiply its impact. It may seem challenging enough to hold on to what you have, but if you're committed to holding on rather than investing in, then that's where to start—by pre-deciding to express your faithfulness by viewing every resource as an opportunity.

This commitment requires you to think ahead in order to hear your Father someday proclaim, "Well done, good and faithful servant! You have been faithful with a few things; I will put you in charge of many things. Come and share your master's happiness!" (Matthew 25:21). This response echoes the words spoken by the master to two of his faithful servants in the parable Jesus told about risking our resources (Matthew 25:14–30). Each of these two servants invested the bags of gold entrusted to them and earned significant dividends.

The third servant's choice, however, and his master's rebuke, reveal what happens when we play it safe:

24 "Then the man who had received one bag of gold came. 'Master,' he said, 'I knew that you are a hard man, harvesting where you have not sown and gathering where you have not scattered seed. 25 So I was afraid and went out and hid your gold in the ground. See, here is what belongs to you.'

[26] "His master replied, 'You wicked, lazy servant! So you knew that I harvest where I have not sown and gather where I have not scattered seed? [27] Well then, you should have put my money on deposit with the bankers, so that when I returned I would have received it back with interest.

[28] "'So take the bag of gold from him and give it to the one who has ten bags. [29] For whoever has will be given more, and they will have an abundance. Whoever does not have, even what they have will be taken from them.'"

Matthew 25:24–29

• Does the harshness of the master's rebuke surprise you? Why do you suppose he's so upset when the third servant actually did think ahead about how upset his master would be if the money was lost?

• Do you agree that it's "wicked" and "lazy" to risk nothing with your resources? How does this motivate you to take greater risks for God's kingdom?

• How would you have responded to the third servant in this situation if the money had been yours? Why?

- Which resources entrusted to you have not been risked and invested for maximum impact? What's kept you from taking greater risks with these resources?

EMBRACING THE TRUTH

Our human tendency to focus on our own needs often gets in the way of recognizing the opportunity we have to add value and multiply impact in the lives of others. Our culture tends to condition us to focus on acquisition and consumption rather than facilitation and generosity. Choosing to be faithful to God requires us to make his concerns our concerns—and his concerns are always about people.

It may feel counterintuitive to hold what you've been given loosely and view it as a resource to be risked in order to be multiplied. You may want to think about what compels you to hold tight to more than you know you need. Because Jesus encouraged his followers not to worry about their future needs and to rely on God to provide for them. Rather than always chasing more, your faithfulness emerges in knowing that you can risk your resources. You don't have to hoard for the future because God will make sure you have everything you need.

[31] "So do not worry, saying, 'What shall we eat?' or 'What shall we drink?' or 'What shall we wear?' [32] For the pagans run after all these things, and your heavenly Father knows that you need them. [33] But seek first his kingdom and his righteousness, and all these things will be given to you as well. [34] Therefore do not worry about tomorrow, for tomorrow will worry about itself. Each day has enough trouble of its own."

MATTHEW 6:31–34

- How often do you find yourself focused on what you lack rather than on what you've been given? What effect does focusing on deprivation rather than abundance have on your faithfulness?

- How does worrying about your future needs undermine your present faith? How do you usually stop yourself from worrying once you realize you're sliding into that mindset?

- When has God most recently met a need for you? When has he most recently prompted you to meet a need for someone else?

- What's one resource you know you need to share more frequently and generously? Who can you bless with this resource today?

CHOOSING HOW YOU CHOOSE

In order to view your resources as opportunities to bless others, you need to be mindful of all you've been given. Conducting a resource inventory of what God has given you to steward is a great way to begin. Some resources may seem obvious based on your education, your job training, your bank account, and your possessions. But try to think beyond these resources and consider your unique experiences, places you've traveled, other languages you speak, your hobbies and interests, or your favorite musicians and sports teams. Everything about you and your life can become a resource when surrendered to God out of faithfulness.

After you've listed as many resources as possible, consider how these could be invested and how their impact could be multiplied. With these opportunities in mind, think about the risk required of you to pursue such successful profits for God's kingdom.

YOUR RESOURCES

Education: _____

Training: _____

Job experience: _____

Skills and abilities: _____

Places you've traveled: _____

Languages you speak: _____

Personal hobbies: _____

Personal passions and interests: _____

Causes and charities you care about: _____

Ministries you've served in: _____

Clubs, teams, and industries you're part of: _____

People groups you know well: _____

People of influence you know: _____

Possessions: _____

Finances: _____

Other resources: _____

_____

Based on this list of resources you've compiled, choose five or six that you want to consider investing and risking for maximum impact. List them below and consider how God might want you to steward them.

Resource	Investment	Possible impact	Risk required
1.			
2.			
3.			
4.			
5.			

DETERMINING YOUR DECISIONS

When God prompts you to do something, you may not immediately recognize the result—or, for that matter, ever entirely know the impact your faithfulness might have. Being sensitive to his prompting usually requires spending time with God and being attuned to his Spirit. This requires eliminating those distractions we discussed in the previous session. With fewer distractions, you can practice stilling your heart before God and listening for his voice. Jesus, our Good Shepherd, said, "My sheep listen to my voice; I know them, and they follow me" (John 10:27).

Discerning God's prompting through the Holy Spirit within you often requires taking action—doing something you might not normally do, giving away something you probably would have held on to, saying something to someone without fully understanding its significance. Or, you may immediately have an understanding of why God is asking you to do what he's prompting you to do or say. Either way, his prompting is an opportunity to demonstrate your faithfulness by being obedient.

Discernment, of course, requires comparing your prompting with what's true about God based on his Word. It also helps to have a certain level of self-awareness and the ability to distinguish between your own various thoughts and the direction of the Spirit. Like many aspects of faithfulness, learning to listen for God's prompting improves with practice and helps you strengthen your trust in the God you love and serve.

- How often do you pause to listen for God's prompting during an average day? How do you discern whether an idea, urge, or risk is from God?

- When was the last time you heard or sensed God's Spirit prompting you to do or say something? How did you respond?

- How have you benefited by someone else acting on the prompting they received from God? What did their words or actions mean to you?

- How willing are you to obey a prompting from God's Spirit even when it does not logically make sense? When it's not convenient or easy?

FREE TO RISK

A life of faith is a life of risk-taking.[20]

CRAIG GROESCHEL

Dan Cates is a professional poker player and winner of two consecutive championship titles at the World Series of Poker held annually in Las Vegas. Now in his early thirties, Cates has won more than $11 million since going pro when he was still a teenager. He cites his moderation in taking risks as the key to both his career and financial success. "You want to push yourself a little, but not too far," Cates explains. "This is always true in everything."[21]

According to Cates, the most successful poker players learn to take appropriate risks while pulling back when necessary. "Push yourself a moderate amount in all aspects," Cates urges. "You want to pursue growth, but pursue it a moderate amount, basically."[22]

Now, clearly, the risk when playing poker varies from the risk taken when you step out in faith in obedience to God (and in no way am I recommending gambling). Playing poker and other forms of gambling rely on chance as much as skill in order to win money for the player. Pre-deciding to be faithful to God by living a life of risk-taking has something much greater at stake—the impact you can have when you add value, maximize your resources, and act on God's prompting.

- Do you enjoy the thrill of taking risks in most areas of your life, or do you usually resist taking risks because they make you so uncomfortable?

- What do you think about Dan Cates's advice to "risk in moderation"? What have you relied on to help you know when to take a risk and when not to risk?

- When have you felt the freedom to risk big for God's kingdom based on recognizing an opportunity and sensing his prompting?

- What often holds you back from taking a leap of faith when you know you need to risk? What are you afraid of?

EXPLORING GOD'S WORD

Life fundamentally requires risk: taking action without knowing exactly what will happen as a result. The life of faith is no exception—and may actually include more and greater risks. If you seek to add value to someone's life, it will mean putting their needs above your own. When you do that, it feels like *risk*.

With multiplying resources, you take necessary risks in order to maximize the return on your investment. As you recall from the parable of the three servants who were entrusted with the bags of gold, their master assumed they would use what he gave them to produce more. When the third servant buried his gold to ensure he wouldn't lose it, his master rebuked him for failing to risk anything. It makes you wonder whether his master would have preferred that this last servant risk his resources and lose some rather than play it safe with no possibility for profit.

Faith requires that we risk—and God continues looking for faithful people. People willing to trust him and step out in faith. To do what may not seem logical or reasonable according to human standards and our mortal senses. God's Word tells us that "without faith it is impossible to please God" (Hebrews 11:6). Which means you cannot play it safe and please God.

Therefore, pre-deciding to live faithfully includes choosing a life of risk-taking. You will see risk as a common denominator in the lives of virtually every person who lived a great life of faith in the Bible. In fact, in Hebrews 11, sometimes called "the faith hall of fame," you find various men and women remembered for their extraordinary faith—which inherently includes the extraordinary risks they took. They knew that it's impossible to be faithful to God and to play it safe.

[1] Now faith is confidence in what we hope for and assurance about what we do not see. [2] This is what the ancients were commended for.

[3] By faith we understand that the universe was formed at God's command, so that what is seen was not made out of what was visible. . . .

[32] And what more shall I say? I do not have time to tell about Gideon, Barak, Samson and Jephthah, about David and Samuel and the prophets, [33] who through faith conquered kingdoms, administered justice, and gained what was promised; who shut the mouths of lions, [34] quenched the fury of the flames, and escaped the edge of the sword; whose weakness was turned to strength; and who became powerful in battle and routed foreign armies. [35] Women received back their dead, raised to life again. There were others who were tortured, refusing to be released so that they might gain an even better resurrection. [36] Some faced jeers and flogging, and even chains and imprisonment. [37] They were put to death by stoning; they were sawed in two; they were killed by the sword. They went about in sheepskins and goatskins, destitute, persecuted and mistreated— [38] the

world was not worthy of them. They wandered in deserts and mountains, living in caves and in holes in the ground.

[39] These were all commended for their faith, yet none of them received what had been promised, [40] since God had planned something better for us so that only together with us would they be made perfect.

HEBREWS 11:1–3, 32–40

- Why do you think there's a correlation between adversity and living by faith in this passage? How do challenges present opportunities for living faithfully?

- Based on the definition of faith at the beginning of this passage, why is risk inherent to living by faith? How does taking a risk demonstrate confidence in what you can't see but know is true?

- Do you agree that "without faith it is impossible to please God" (Hebrews 11:6)? Do you then agree that as you live out your faith without risk, it is impossible to please God?

- Choose your favorite Bible translation and read verses 4 through 31 in Hebrews 11. Which of the giants of the faith listed stands out to you right now? Why?

EMBRACING THE TRUTH

As the author of Hebrews points out at the end of describing these men and women of extraordinary faith (11:39–40), none of them received the fulfillment of what they had been promised during their lifetime. Why? Because "God had planned something better for us so that only together with us would they be made perfect" (Hebrews 11:40). These individuals trusted in God and demonstrated amazing faithfulness despite not experiencing all that God promised them until Jesus came, died on the cross, and rose again.

Their willingness to believe God without necessarily understanding or seeing with their human eyes what he was doing reminds us once again of the risk involved. We can rely on what we observe and experience with our mortal senses, or we can dare to believe in the invisible spiritual realities identified and described in God's Word: "For our struggle is not against flesh and blood, but against the rulers, against the authorities, against the powers of this dark world and against the spiritual forces of evil in the heavenly realms" (Ephesians 6:12).

Whatever you rely on as the basis for living your life requires risk. You can continue making decisions rationally and logically, which is nonetheless subjective. Or, you can dare to trust the God of the universe and follow the example of his Son, Jesus, through the power of his Holy Spirit.

- When have you been faithful to take a risk and seen the result? How did knowing you were part of this result affect your view of the way God often works?

- When have you been reluctant or chosen not to risk by faith because you could not imagine any possible positive outcome? How willing are you to relinquish control and just obey God without understanding the reasons behind it?

- If your name were someday added to the faith hall of fame in Hebrews 11, what would you be known for? What have you already overcome by faith that demonstrates God's power, love, and purpose in your life?

- How many big risks of faith do you estimate taking in your life so far? What has to change in your life in order for your faith legacy to be one based on risk?

CHOOSING HOW YOU CHOOSE

If risk-taking does not come naturally for you, it might seem unfair for God to seemingly ask more of you than others who enjoy the thrill of taking risks. Regardless of how faithful risk-taking makes you feel, everyone who follows God must deal with uncertainty. Of course, everyone who doesn't follow God faces uncertainty as well. But most of the time we live our lives based on what seems probable and predictable based on past experiences and certain assumptions and conclusions we've drawn.

The only problem is that we often form false assumptions and inaccurate conclusions. Because we don't know all the variables, details, events, relationships, and motives in what unfolds around us, we try to close the gaps between what we know and what we don't know by inference. Our brains are wired to connect dots in order to help us process data, learn information, and avoid past mistakes. But we all know that our emotions can get in the way, and we form beliefs around what we feel, perceive, and assume.

When it comes to risks of any kind, we may be biased against them because we associate them with past times when we risked being vulnerable only to face rejection. Or we may have risked being generous but never received acknowledgment, let alone a thank-you. We might have gone for a promotion we felt like God wanted us to move into, only to be overlooked in favor of someone less qualified and experienced. In order to become more comfortable with faithful risk-taking, it's good to recognize your current associations, perspectives, and biases.

With this goal in mind, complete the following:

- False assumptions about risk:

- Inaccurate conclusions about risk:

- Personal biases toward or against risk:

- What God says is true about risk:

DETERMINING YOUR DECISIONS

Experiencing the freedom to risk by faith comes with practice. It also requires a commitment to continue acting on what you've pre-decided based on what you know God expects from you. Living faithfully never happens by accident but by being intentional in how you steward the resources, opportunities, and relationships entrusted to you.

Remember, as you are faithful in each small risk, God will trust you with more. Your responsibility is to be obedient—not to control the outcome. Trust God with the outcome. You may overestimate what he can do in the short run with the risks you take, but you will vastly underestimate what God can do through a lifetime of your faithfulness.

As you consider what it means for you to be more faithful by being more of a risk-taker, let's identify some specific ways you can move forward. Use the following prompts to help you reflect:

Probably the biggest faith-risk I've ever taken was _____
_____
_____ .

What I learned about God from taking that big risk was _____
_____
_____ .

What I learned about myself, my fears, and my doubts was _____
_____
_____ .

One person with whom I believe God wants me to risk more is _____
_____
_____ .

One resource currently entrusted to me that I know God can use for more is
_____
_____ .

The next big risk of faith I want to take most likely involves _____
_____
_____ .

I WILL BE AN INFLUENCER

Being faithful means using your influence to help others experience God's grace and the love of Jesus. By recognizing the impact you have on those around you, you pre-decide to pray, lead by example, and speak truth in love. By shaping your decisions on the opportunities for influence you have, you become salt and light in the world, adding flavor and bringing light. Deciding to make the most of your influence requires risk as you look for opportunities around you and act on them for God's kingdom. Here are the key principles you will learn in part 4:

- Jesus said, "Go into the world and shine," not "go into your homes and hide."
- To be salt and light, you can pre-decide to influence with your prayers, your example, and your words.
- Prayer focuses your attention on opportunities you have to help others experience the grace of God and the love of Jesus.
- If you want to effect change in people's lives by *pointing* them to Jesus, start by *praying* for them.
- When you know who you are, you know what to do and how to influence by example.
- When you live out being salt and light, people notice and are changed.
- You are an influencer, and God wants to use you.
- Knowing how patient and persistent God has been with you, show others that same patience and persistence.

I WILL INFLUENCE WITH MY PRAYERS

Salt and light find their purpose when they come in direct contact with food and darkness.[23]

CRAIG GROESCHEL

Social media influencers continue to impact retail sales for virtually any and every product. Some influencers simply promote the products of their advertisers or sponsors. Others pride themselves on being independent and only recommend the items that they themselves have tested and use regularly. Still others bring followers along as they try out certain products within a particular niche.

Such is the case with travel blogger Cory Lee, who focuses specifically on travel for people with limitations and disabilities. Diagnosed with spinal muscular atrophy at age two, Cory grew up using a wheelchair but never allowed it to stop him from enjoying his love of travel. As more people began asking for Cory's travel advice and recommendations, he started his blog, *Curb Free with Cory Lee*. He explains his mission is "to show you how to travel, where to travel, and most importantly, *why* travel as a person with a disability."[24]

In 2021, Winnebago, an iconic brand in recreational vehicles, provided Cory with a new Winnebago Specialty Vehicle designed for travelers requiring wheelchairs or who have other special needs. In exchange for blogging and posting about his experiences, Cory was sponsored by Winnebago to travel across the country. The highly successful partnership reached more than 16,000 followers and included over 47,000 unique impressions. Winnebago picked up three times as many followers to their social media accounts as compared to a similar sponsored trip the prior year.[25]

You don't have to be on social media, though, to wield significant influence.

Pre-deciding to be an influencer allows you to leverage something considerably more impactful than social media—the power of prayer.

- How many social media influencers do you regularly follow? How often do you make a purchase because of an online recommendation from an influencer?

- What qualities or characteristics make you more likely to trust the recommendations of an online influencer? Why?

- How often do you post reviews and recommendations online? Do you consider yourself a social media influencer?

- Who are the people who wield the most influence in your life right now? Why do you trust them to allow their influence to affect you?

EXPLORING GOD'S WORD

Jesus made it clear that we have something the world needs. He compared what we bring to salt—used for centuries as both a flavoring and a preservative—and to light—used since God created the heavens and the earth to illuminate darkness. Salt fulfills its purpose when it comes in direct contact with food. Light naturally illuminates any darkness surrounding it.

As followers of Jesus intent on making the best decisions, we recognize our influence. And we pre-decide to use our influence to glorify God, to point others to Jesus, and to advance God's kingdom. In his teaching known as the "Sermon on the Mount," Jesus urged his followers to realize that what they bring to the world does no good until it's in the midst of those who need it most.

[13] "You are the salt of the earth. But if the salt loses its saltiness, how can it be made salty again? It is no longer good for anything, except to be thrown out and trampled underfoot.

[14] "You are the light of the world. A town built on a hill cannot be hidden. [15] Neither do people light a lamp and put it under a bowl. Instead they put it on its stand, and it gives light to everyone in the house. [16] In the same way, let your light shine before others, that they may see your good deeds and glorify your Father in heaven."

MATTHEW 5:13–16

- What do salt and light have in common with those of us who follow Jesus? What do we add when we choose to use our influence for God's purposes?

- What happens to followers who don't use what they have to flavor and illuminate their surroundings? What's lost when believers withhold themselves?

- How comfortable are you being the center of attention? Is calling attention to yourself essential to being salt and light?

- How would you describe the flavor of your faith in God? How does your flavor of faith season those with whom you interact?

EMBRACING THE TRUTH

You may be tempted to overlook how much influence you wield through your prayers. Depending on when and how often you pray, you might not feel you spend enough time praying for other people. When you recognize your prayers make a difference—for them and for you—it's more than worth the time and deliberation required to make praying for others something you've pre-decided to do.

Being sensitive to the voice of God's Spirit, you may often have someone unexpectedly come to mind. You may not even know their need or their name, only that God has brought them to mind. While you may feel prompted to do more for them, you can certainly begin to add value simply by praying for them.

In addition to praying for the needs of others, you will also want to pray for other believers and the influence they exert. Prayers of protection and victory over the enemy are also significant ways we can influence and empower one another as we seek to be salt and light.

> [2] Devote yourselves to prayer, being watchful and thankful. [3] And pray for us, too, that God may open a door for our message, so that we may proclaim the mystery of Christ, for which I am in chains. [4] Pray that I may proclaim it clearly, as I should. [5] Be wise in the way you act toward outsiders; make the most of every opportunity. [6] Let your conversation be always full of grace, seasoned with salt, so that you may know how to answer everyone.
>
> COLOSSIANS 4:2–6

- Who are the people you tend to pray for regularly? How often do you ask them for prayer requests or check in with them about what they need?

- Who are the people you see or interact with regularly who also need your prayers? Who in particular do you want to be intentional about praying for over the next few weeks?

- Who are some brothers and sisters in Christ whose influence you admire? Why are you drawn to the way they relate to others?

- Who can you ask for a prayer request today that will stretch you out of your comfort zone? How can praying for others allow you to risk in faithfulness?

CHOOSING HOW YOU CHOOSE

No matter how introverted or homebound you may be, technology allows everyone to have more influence than ever before. You don't have to be an official influencer to find ways to connect, respond, and encourage others online. Whether you send a text to let a friend know you're praying for them or post a response that questions a popular opinion, you reflect Christ by offering salt and light.

Most people not only have the capability to be a faith-influencer online but also across their various network of relationships, interactions, and affiliations. You may not realize how vast your influence is until you consider how many different people, groups, teams, and families you touch in your life right now. While you may not have obvious opportunities to share your faith or discuss spiritual things, you can still pray for them and remain vigilant when such opportunities eventually emerge.

Spend a few moments in prayer, stilling your heart before God and asking the Holy Spirit to speak and direct you according to his will and purposes. Then brainstorm the various connections you have and the influence you wield, using the questions and prompts below.

FAMILY MEMBERS

- Who are the family members, both immediate and extended, you influence regularly? Write their names below and then, beside each, name a specific need or item you can pray for them.

Name:	What/how you can pray for them:

COWORKERS, COLLEAGUES, BOSSES, PEERS

- Who are the career, work, and job-related individuals with whom you have some influence? List them below and ways you can pray for them.

Name:	What/how you can pray for them:

NEIGHBORS, FRIENDS, COMMUNITY MEMBERS

- What about neighbors, friends, or community members you know well enough to have an influence on? How can you pray for them?

Name:	What/how you can pray for them:

CONNECTIONS, ACQUAINTANCES, SERVICE PROVIDERS

● Finally, what about those special connections, familiar acquaintances, and service providers? List their names and how you can pray for them.

Name:	What/how you can pray for them:

DETERMINING YOUR DECISIONS

Choosing to take risks in order to wield the influence you have with others often becomes, well, risky. You may recall the experience I describe in chapter 4.1 of *Think Ahead* in which I agreed to meet a well-known (and not necessarily for good reasons) community member for lunch and ended up sitting at the bar in a popular, crowded restaurant. Before I got back to my office at the church, two informants had called to tattle on what they had heard or witnessed.

Basically, as I pointed out, you can choose to be someone who eats with sinners—you know, the people others tend to judge, condemn, criticize, or hold strong opinions about—or you can refrain from hanging out with others who have a bad reputation in order not to give anyone the idea that you've slipped in your faith and now do the same things these people are known for doing.

Either way, you can't control what other people will think and say about you. So why not follow the example Jesus set for us? Which is to err on the side of relationship.

- Have you ever been in a situation where you felt like you were in the wrong place for the right reasons? Did you receive criticism or comments from others about taking this risk?

- Would you be (or have you been) willing to meet someone in a bar or other establishment you don't normally frequent in order to deepen your relationship?

- What are some boundaries you refuse to cross in terms of "eating with sinners" and being salt and light in the world?

- Who is someone you know whom others tend to judge or criticize? Write out a prayer for this person that includes your willingness to meet with them and talk with them about the love of Jesus.

I WILL INFLUENCE WITH MY EXAMPLE AND WORDS

Because you are a light, you don't run from the darkness, you shine in it. . . . Because you are salt, you don't run from the impurities, you cleanse them, and God uses you as an agent of change.[26]

CRAIG GROESCHEL

Never underestimate the influence you can have on others simply by showing up.

Writer Nancy Fidler tells about how her father, who suffered from Parkinson's disease, worked as a special ed teacher at a Chicago high school in their neighborhood. For nearly thirty years after his diagnosis, Mr. Fidler continued to teach and love his students, treating them with the same respect, dignity, and compassion he believed every student deserved.[27]

By the time he was in his sixties, Mr. Fidler often struggled with the pain, fatigue, and consequences caused by Parkinson's but continued to persevere. One morning when he went to the school, he lost his balance going up some stairs and fell. Despite being sore and bruised, he didn't consider going home and proceeded to teach his classes. Throughout the day he began to feel better and walk normally with more pep in his step.

This caught the attention of a teen student who popped into his classroom at the end of the day. She wasn't in any of Mr. Fidler's classes, but she recognized him and knew about his illness. She had witnessed his fall on the stairs that morning as well as the way he immediately got up and continued on. When she spotted him in between classes, she noticed that he seemed undeterred by his fall and eventually began walking as he normally did. So at the end of the day, she stepped into his classroom and told Mr. Fidler, "I just want to say thank you for saving my life."[28]

She went on to explain her depression and battle with suicidal thoughts. This young woman had begun the morning intending to take her own life. But observing Mr. Fidler's example of strength and perseverance through suffering inspired her to keep going. "I then realized that everything will get better as the days go on," she concluded.

Mr. Fidler had no idea of the way his example had influenced this student. When he shared the story with his daughter Nancy, she was not surprised. Her father's example had been inspiring her for her entire life.

- When has someone else's example helped you get through a tough day or challenging season? Did they realize they were inspiring you to persevere?

- How much does another person's example influence the way you act? At work, for instance, how much does someone else's example of leadership impact your own?

- How aware are you of setting an example for those around you on a daily basis? If you asked them, how would they describe the example you set?

- How would you describe the example you want to set for everyone around you? What sometimes interferes with your attempt to set this kind of example?

EXPLORING GOD'S WORD

Sometimes our examples have the greatest impact on those in need of acceptance, understanding, compassion, and hope. People tend to notice how others treat them, with their attitude and words as well as their body language and actions. If you're paying attention, you've probably spotted this kind of communication within seconds of talking to a waitress, cashier, or customer service rep. Their job requires them to serve you, but depending on a variety of factors, they may not be eager to serve.

In those moments, the opportunity shifts to you and your example. Regardless of the message you're receiving from them, you can decide to make your interaction one that surprises them by adding value or one that reinforces their bias against customers in your demographic. You can make it a power struggle to emphasize that you as the customer should always be right.

Or, you can make it a relational interaction that reflects how Jesus engaged with people—surprising them with respect, grace, and the truth told in love. This is the example we see in his encounter with someone who never imagined the impact a drink of water could have on their lives.

[7] When a Samaritan woman came to draw water, Jesus said to her, "Will you give me a drink?" [8] (His disciples had gone into the town to buy food.)

⁹ The Samaritan woman said to him, "You are a Jew and I am a Samaritan woman. How can you ask me for a drink?" (For Jews do not associate with Samaritans.)

¹⁰ Jesus answered her, "If you knew the gift of God and who it is that asks you for a drink, you would have asked him and he would have given you living water."

¹¹ "Sir," the woman said, "you have nothing to draw with and the well is deep. Where can you get this living water? ¹² Are you greater than our father Jacob, who gave us the well and drank from it himself, as did also his sons and his livestock?"

¹³ Jesus answered, "Everyone who drinks this water will be thirsty again, ¹⁴ but whoever drinks the water I give them will never thirst. Indeed, the water I give them will become in them a spring of water welling up to eternal life."

¹⁵ The woman said to him, "Sir, give me this water so that I won't get thirsty and have to keep coming here to draw water."

¹⁶ He told her, "Go, call your husband and come back."

¹⁷ "I have no husband," she replied.

Jesus said to her, "You are right when you say you have no husband. ¹⁸ The fact is, you have had five husbands, and the man you now have is not your husband. What you have just said is quite true."

¹⁹ "Sir," the woman said, "I can see that you are a prophet. ²⁰ Our ancestors worshiped on this mountain, but you Jews claim that the place where we must worship is in Jerusalem."

²¹ "Woman," Jesus replied, "believe me, a time is coming when you will worship the Father neither on this mountain nor in Jerusalem. ²² You Samaritans worship what you do not know; we worship what we do know, for salvation is from the Jews. ²³ Yet a time is coming and has now come when the true worshipers will worship the Father in the Spirit and in truth, for they are the kind of worshipers the Father seeks. ²⁴ God is spirit, and his worshipers must worship in the Spirit and in truth."

²⁵ The woman said, "I know that Messiah" (called Christ) "is coming. When he comes, he will explain everything to us."

²⁶ Then Jesus declared, "I, the one speaking to you—I am he."

JOHN 4:7–26

- What message did Jesus convey to the Samaritan woman merely by speaking to her? How did his request change her expectations about their interaction?

- Why do you suppose Jesus compared what he offered to living water? How does the Samaritan woman initially interpret this offer?

- Why do you suppose Jesus does not confront the woman about her husbands and current relationship status? How does his lack of condemnation redirect the woman's attention?

- How does the example Jesus set in this encounter inspire you to see others beyond their appearance or first impression?

EMBRACING THE TRUTH

Following the example Jesus set often compels us to cross social and cultural barriers and to disrupt stereotypes. Sometimes people respond, similar to the way the Samaritan woman initially responded to Jesus, by wearing the labels others have given them. Because so many others have spoken to them or acted certain ways, they assume you will as well. Which is where the brilliance of Jesus' divine relational style can inspire us.

We can't ignore that certain boundaries, stereotypes, and prejudices exist. So recognizing the treatment others have likely received can help you see them beyond the labels and demographics. Most people continue to be surprised when another person pauses to listen, to look, and to know them for who they really are. Rather than trying to convince them of anything or get something from them, you wield considerable influence simply by being present and looking beyond surface appearances, social context, and cultural assumptions.

- Who are the people you tend to avoid or feel uncomfortable around? How can you show them the love of Jesus simply by your attitude?

- When have you recently interacted with another person whom you assumed was very different from you in their beliefs and lifestyle? How would you describe your interaction with them?

- What are some ways you can acknowledge social and cultural labels on others without succumbing to them in your words and example?

- Who is someone you see regularly but have not gotten to know because you assume, for whatever reasons, they're not interested? How can you take a first step toward engaging with this person?

CHOOSING HOW YOU CHOOSE

When you pre-decide to be an influencer, you choose your words carefully and think before you act. While surprising others with how we relate can get their attention, you want to make sure it's a favorable surprise. You don't need to have a script you follow or memorize Bible verses to quote. You simply need to be yourself and show others that you genuinely care about them.

Just as Jesus interacted with the woman at the well, you want to relate to others, regardless of their differences or similarities to you, with respect, grace, and kindness. Jesus used his words to engage the Samaritan woman in conversation, surprising her with his disregard for the cultural boundaries of her ethnicity and gender. When he offered her living water and revealed his identity as the long-awaited Messiah, Jesus kept the focus on the woman and her needs—not on his sovereignty, righteousness, or power. He remained relational and offered grace and mercy instead of shame and judgment.

What's also striking in their encounter is how the Samaritan woman then immediately left her water jar, returned to town, and used her words to offer testimony about meeting Jesus: "Come, see a man who told me everything I ever did. Could this be the Messiah?" (John 4:29). And how did they respond? "They came out of the town and made their way toward him" (John 4:30).

Without shame or hesitation, she acknowledged her tarnished reputation and shared how Jesus told her everything she ever did. Instead of demanding or urging others to believe in Christ, she asked the same question she herself had just finished asking: "Could this be the Messiah?" Asking questions rather than proclaiming statements—even ones that are true—often invites others to engage rather than causing them to put up defenses. Townspeople gathered and began to head toward Jesus simply because this woman spoke up.

Her words led others to encounter Christ for themselves, and the results changed their lives: "Many of the Samaritans from that town believed in him because of the woman's testimony. . . . They said to the woman, 'We no longer believe just because of what you said; now we have heard for ourselves, and we know that this man really is the Savior of the world'" (John 4:39, 42).

You have the opportunity to speak up as well. Just as she saw an opportunity to share her Jesus-encounter with others, you can look for moments when it's natural to let others know what Jesus means to you. You can also look for opportunities to invite your friends, neighbors, and coworkers to a church service, holiday event, or small group where they can encounter Jesus more directly.

You don't have to be a good speaker, have a large platform, or have your life together to influence others by telling them about Jesus. You simply have to speak up.

- What often prevents you from speaking up and telling others about your faith? Are you more concerned about knowing what to say or about how others might respond?

- How does the Samaritan woman's example strike you? What can you learn from the simple way she let others know about what had happened in her life because of meeting Jesus?

- When was the last time you spoke candidly about your faith in God with a friend, colleague, neighbor, or acquaintance? What prompted you to speak up?

- When was the last time you invited someone to visit your church, attend a faith-related event, or check out your small group?

DETERMINING YOUR DECISIONS

Pre-deciding to use your influence by praying, speaking, and setting an example requires patience. While you remain vigilant for everyday opportunities to influence others around you, many times your cumulative testimony has a greater impact. Rarely does a one-time conversation or exchange lead someone to accept Christ. More often, their decision is the result of relationships developed over time.

When you live out being salt and light, gradually people will notice and be curious. When you let your light shine, they will be attracted to the light. They will want what you have. And then you can share your greatest treasure more directly. You can help them know—through what you say and what you do—the unconditional love of God displayed through his sinless son, Jesus.

So remember, influence is often a long game. When you're tempted to give up on someone, don't stop praying. Don't stop believing. And don't give up. You are salt and light. You run into the darkness, and you shine the love of Jesus into it. God made you to make a difference, and you need to just be who you are.

You have influence—and you know how to use it.

- Who are the nonbelievers with a front-row seat to your life right now? How is your example influencing them?

- Who have you stopped engaging or interacting with because they seemed uninterested or hostile to your faith? While respecting their wishes, how can you continue to befriend them?

- Who have you been praying for over a long period of time in hopes you can share your faith with them? What's a next step you can take toward getting closer to them?

- How will you be more intentional in using your influence now than you would have a month ago? Why?

PART 5

I WILL BE GENEROUS

Choosing to be generous reflects your faithfulness and reliance on God as the source for everything you need. By pre-deciding that you will be generous, you reflect God's goodness to those around you, countering the cultural conditioning to acquire, receive, and consume. Your generosity reflects what you have received from God as you become a conduit for his generosity in the lives of others. Generosity becomes who you are and emerges in what you do. Pre-deciding to act generously in all you do, you demonstrate your trust in God. Here are the key principles you will learn in part 5:

- Our culture tells us it is more blessed to get; Jesus said you will be blessed more when you give (Acts 20:35).
- Generosity is not about what you have or don't have, but about your heart.
- If you're not generous now, you won't be generous later. More money doesn't change who you are; it just reveals who you are.
- If you want to be generous when you have more, learn to be generous when you have less.
- Giving is not just what you do; giving is who you are.
- Generosity is intentional, strategic, and driven by a desire to honor God and live the kind of life he blesses.
- Generosity allows faith to replace fear and blessing to replace worry.
- You cannot outgive God.
- Knowing that generosity never happens by accident, you pre-decide to stand firm in your generosity regardless of your circumstances.

HOW TO BE MORE BLESSED

You'll have more happiness when you become more generous.[29]

CRAIG GROESCHEL

The billion-dollar self-help industry—yes, it's so pervasive and lucrative that it's become a recognized industry—may not be helping as many selves as you'd expect. In fact, according to some experts, self-help products, such as books and seminars, may actually have a harmful impact on people seeking positivity, motivation, and self-confidence. A recent study revealed that frequent readers of self-help books had higher levels of cortisol, the hormone released when the human body is stressed, than average. They also tended to struggle with symptoms of depression more than nonreaders of self-help material.[30]

Psychologist Mark Travers, PhD, believes part of the problem with popular self-help material is "a one-size-fits-all approach to mental health." Compared to personal therapy and counseling, Travers points out, mass-market self-help content fails to personalize the information and instruction provided. "When you approach a mental health practitioner for help, they listen to you, understand you, and offer solutions that work for your unique situation. On the contrary, when someone writes a self-help book, their goal is to sell to as many people as they can."[31]

The other problem with general self-help material is the additional pressure many people experience when reading and hearing about what others seem to have done successfully that they cannot. Today, many self-help gurus base their content on science and neurology. Instead of being perceived as con artists or slick promise-sellers, these authors, speakers, and life coaches have highly reputable medical, academic, and entrepreneurial backgrounds. They offer what appear to be proven methods, leaving those unable to succeed with their techniques feeling more discouraged.[32]

Nonetheless, people will continue looking for ways to find peace, fulfillment, purpose, meaning, health, and well-being in their lives. You know this is a spiritual longing only Jesus can fill. And he told us that the key to being blessed is to be a blessing to others.

- How often do you tend to read a self-help book, watch a video, or attend a seminar? What has been your general experience with self-help material?

- Have you ever engaged with a self-help product only to feel disappointed or discouraged afterward? Why did you feel this way?

- Do you believe that Christians can benefit from most self-help content? Or does it depend on its faith content and the beliefs of the author?

- How would you describe what it feels like when you're being blessed by someone else? When you are blessing someone else?

EXPLORING GOD'S WORD

Thinking ahead and pre-deciding to be a generous person reflects the character of God and the example set by Jesus. Just because you're a believer, though, does not mean generosity will automatically come easier for you. You'll recall from chapter 5.1 in *Think Ahead* how humans are wired to underestimate our own selfishness in comparison to others. In other words, we may think we're being generous, even selfless, but objectively we're not. Cultural conditioning also reminds us constantly that we cannot be happy without material gain. The problem, however, is that enough is never enough.

Which is why generosity may seem countercultural or even counterintuitive. But God's Word remains consistently clear about using what he's entrusted to us to bless others, meet their needs, and advance his kingdom. We are merely stewards, not permanent owners, of everything we have. When we hold our blessings loosely and give generously, we discover the joy of being more like Christ. We realize the truth of what Jesus said, that earthly treasure will not last—it's subject to decay, theft, and fire. Heavenly treasure, however, endures forever (Matthew 6:19–21).

Remember, "where your treasure is, there your heart will be also"(Matthew 6:21). When you faithfully risk and invest what you've been given, you will be entrusted with more. The more you receive, the more you have to give. Once you begin experiencing this reality, you discover that no feeling on earth compares to giving away what you cannot keep.

6 Remember this: Whoever sows sparingly will also reap sparingly, and whoever sows generously will also reap generously. 7 Each of you should give what you have decided in your heart to give, not reluctantly or under compulsion, for God loves a cheerful giver. 8 And God is able to bless you

abundantly, so that in all things at all times, having all that you need, you will abound in every good work. . . . [11] You will be enriched in every way so that you can be generous on every occasion, and through us your generosity will result in thanksgiving to God.

2 CORINTHIANS 9:6–8, 11

- What does it mean to you to be a "cheerful giver"? Why do you suppose God does not want us to give "reluctantly or under compulsion"?

- On a scale of 1 to 10, with 1 being "It's all mine!" and 10 being "I'm giving it all away!", how would you rate your generosity? What's the basis for your score?

- When has God provided what you needed through the generosity of others? How did this experience reinforce the last half of this passage?

- What do you struggle with giving away? Right now is it easier to give money or to give your time and attention?

EMBRACING THE TRUTH

Deciding to be generous includes a willingness to give all you have. This does not necessarily mean you give away everything God has entrusted to you all at once. Or, it might, depending on his prompting. When giving generously, you're usually forced to trust that God will meet all your needs even as your generosity may be meeting needs for others. If this style of generosity sounds extreme, just remember what Jesus said after witnessing a relatively small gift being made by someone:

> [1] As Jesus looked up, he saw the rich putting their gifts into the temple treasury. [2] He also saw a poor widow put in two very small copper coins. [3] "Truly I tell you," he said, "this poor widow has put in more than all the others. [4] All these people gave their gifts out of their wealth; but she out of her poverty put in all she had to live on."
>
> LUKE 21:1-4

- Why do you suppose Jesus said that this widow's meager gift—two small coins—had more value than all the other gifts given that day?

- How would you explain the difference between sacrificial generosity and giving out of one's wealth? Why is generosity relative to what you have been entrusted to steward?

- When have you given sacrificially in order to bless others? What were you giving up in order to practice generosity?

- What stands out most to you about the scene in the temple that Jesus witnessed?

CHOOSING HOW YOU CHOOSE

If you struggle with being generous, you may sometimes think, *Once I have more and get out of debt, I'll give more. Then I'll be in a place where I can afford to be more generous.* Or you tell yourself, "I'm as generous now as I can afford to be based on what I earn. Eventually, as my earning power increases and my savings add up, then I'll give more."

Sadly, if this is the case, then you're not telling yourself the truth.

Generosity does not seem to work this way for anyone, regardless of their beliefs or income level. As it turns out, generosity is not about what you have or don't have. Generosity is about your heart. Which explains why Jesus valued the gift given by the poor widow in the temple. She gave all she had—without a safety net, savings, or a 401(k). She demonstrated her faith in God to meet her needs by giving all she could possibly give.

You have likely observed the truth of this in action. You've seen poor people who are stingy and other impoverished people who, like the widow Jesus saw, give extravagantly and sacrificially. You also know of wealthy people who are changing the world with intentional, open-handed generosity, and rich people who aren't willing to give anything at all.

Generosity is not about how much you have; it's about your heart.

You may think you would give more if you made more, but studies consistently show that people who make more also spend more. Their purchasing power and level of consumption rises to match their increased income. Or they save more and invest the rest. They don't suddenly become generous once they have more money.

Having more money never made anyone more generous. Having more money simply reveals more of who you are and what you value. If you're not generous now, you will not be generous when you win the lottery. Generosity is never about your finances—generosity is about your heart.

- Based on your experience and observations, do you agree that having more does not determine generosity?

- Have you experienced a time when you unexpectedly had more money? How did you handle your windfall?

- Can you think of people you know who demonstrate generosity despite having meager means to give? How about people who clearly seem to prioritize wealth accumulation over generosity?

- What does generosity look like for you in your current season of life?

DETERMINING YOUR DECISIONS

Your views of generosity, like most other character traits and qualities, have probably been shaped at least in part by the examples and attitudes you were taught growing up. If your parents and family practiced generosity regardless of what they had or didn't have, then you likely learned the joy of being generous as a worthwhile practice. On the other hand, if your family and primary caregivers struggled financially, worried about money, and reinforced a sense of deprivation, then you may view generosity as a luxury for people who have more.

For most people, money has an emotional and psychological charge to it. We live in societies and cultures with economies that promote accumulating wealth, often in order to be more independent and to enjoy more of whatever money can buy. Fear, anxiety, stress, and worry are sparked when we struggle to have enough to pay our bills and purchase the items we consider necessities. We may view wealthy people with envy and assume that they have it made and never worry or struggle in their relationship with money.

In order to pre-decide to practice God-glorifying, outrageous generosity, you may need to examine some of your associations, beliefs, and assumptions about money and how it's used. Under the spotlight of what God says is true and what he promises us, you may discover that now is a good time to reconsider your perspective on money, finances, and wealth. So spend a few moments in prayer, asking God to give you wisdom and discernment, and then reflect on your relationship with money by asking yourself the questions below.

- What were the lessons or principles you learned about money growing up?

- Who did they come from and how were they reinforced?

- What has been the impact of these lessons on how you view money now?

- Which lessons do you feel need to be revised by God's truth or eliminated from your thinking?

STANDING FIRM IN GENEROSITY

Generous people pre-decide to round up. . . . They strategically orient their lives around the value of blessing others.[33]

CRAIG GROESCHEL

Jeff Bezos is now renowned as one of the world's wealthiest people, estimated at well over $100 billion thanks to the incomparable success of Amazon, which he founded in 1994. Less well-known is the name of his former wife of twenty-five years, MacKenzie Scott, who consistently avoids attention even as she proceeds to be one of the most generous philanthropists in history. Since their divorce in 2019, Ms. Scott has quietly donated more than $14 billion to over 1,600 nonprofits "to use as they see fit for the benefit of others," according to her website.[34]

An Ivy League-educated writer who studied with Nobel Prize winner Toni Morrison, Ms. Scott came from a life of privilege but almost dropped out of college when her family lost their assets and filed for bankruptcy. A friend willing to loan her tuition money convinced her to finish her degree, which she did. After graduation Ms. Scott took an entry-level job at a financial firm in New York, hired by the man she would soon marry, Jeff Bezos.

The couple soon moved to Seattle to fulfill Bezos's dream of launching the online retailer that would eventually dominate the market. They used all their personal savings, along with loans from family and investors, to launch Amazon. Apparently, they weren't always sure how they would pay their rent, but within a relatively short few years, the success of the online juggernaut ensured that they would never have to answer that question again.

Awarded cash and Amazon stock from their divorce settlement fluctuating around $50 billion, Ms. Scott immediately set out to give away as much as responsibly possible. Committed to maintaining her privacy and living her life out of the media's glare, she has nonetheless been clear about her objective as a philanthropist. Less than a year after her divorce, Ms. Scott publicly stated on the website for The Giving Pledge, an organization started by Bill Gates and Warren Buffett to encourage billionaires to give away at least half their wealth, that she promised to "keep at it until the safe is empty."[35]

In the almost five years since then, she continues to fulfill her promise.

- What's your take on the promise made by MacKenzie Scott to give away her considerable fortune? What surprises you about her?

- What does Ms. Scott's style of giving reveal about her understanding of generosity? How does her definition of generosity compare to your own?

- Do you think it likely that she was known for being generous prior to her wealth? Why or why not?

- How would you go about giving away billions of dollars if they were yours to give? Who or what would be one of the first recipients of your windfall?

EXPLORING GOD'S WORD

Generosity requires a commitment. And a commitment to generosity requires strategic pre-decisions about how you will exercise and sustain your generosity. Generous people make a plan with their finances and resources that ensures they give consistently. They look for opportunities to round up and give more than is requested or expected. And they think ahead and make sure their generosity is a fundamental part of their lifestyle, not one-off decisions depending on their income and circumstances. Basically, even in their generosity they're extra-generous.

This type of kindness, forethought, and above-and-beyond giving emerges in a parable Jesus told as part of a conversation with an expert in the law. When the command to "love your neighbor as yourself" came up, this man asked Jesus whom he should consider his neighbor.

[30] In reply Jesus said: "A man was going down from Jerusalem to Jericho, when he was attacked by robbers. They stripped him of his clothes, beat him and went away, leaving him half dead. [31] A priest happened to be going down the same road, and when he saw the man, he passed by on the other side. [32] So too, a Levite, when he came to the place and saw him, passed by on the other side. [33] But a Samaritan, as he traveled, came where the man was; and when he saw him, he took pity on him. [34] He went to him and bandaged his wounds, pouring on oil and wine. Then he put the man on his own donkey, brought him to an inn and took care of him. [35] The next day he took out two denarii and gave them to the innkeeper. 'Look after him,' he said, 'and when I return, I will reimburse you for any extra expense you may have.'

³⁶ "Which of these three do you think was a neighbor to the man who fell into the hands of robbers?"

³⁷ The expert in the law replied, "The one who had mercy on him."

Jesus told him, "Go and do likewise."

LUKE 10:30–37

- Why do you suppose Jesus included other passersby in the parable? Why did he identify them as a priest and a Levite—familiar Jewish religious leaders?

- How does the Samaritan go above and beyond and round up his generosity to the man who was robbed and beaten?

- What plan does the Samaritan put in place in order to sustain his generosity in his absence? What does this reveal about his willingness to meet the needs of the wounded man?

- What resonates most for you in this parable? How does it inspire you to be more generous in loving your neighbors—even those you're not supposed to like?

EMBRACING THE TRUTH

In our age of scams, hacked accounts, and deceptive manipulation, you might understandably feel skeptical at times when encountering someone in need. You may have seen someone on a busy street corner with a homemade sign, declaring themselves homeless and asking for money one day, and then driving around in a new truck the next. You might have fallen for an online scam where an individual who claimed to be someone you knew said that they were in desperate need of funds to get home or to pay emergency medical bills. Perhaps you donated money to pay for cancer treatment for someone you followed on social media, only to discover later that they were arrested for fraud.

While it's true that you should use good judgment and biblical discernment, there will inevitably be situations where you're not sure whether someone's need is legitimate or not. Or you might wonder whether their need is greater than someone else's you know about, or even your own. In the midst of those moments, however, is not the time to decide. Generosity blankets who you are and flows from the attitude of your heart. There might be times when your generosity is exploited, but that is on the conscience of the one who misled you. Your generosity reflects your reliance on, trust in, and love of God.

When your relationship with the Lord is the basis for your generosity, you love giving just to glorify his goodness and to draw others to him. This is the motivation we see mentioned in describing the early believers in the churches of ancient Macedonia:

> [1] Now I want you to know, dear brothers and sisters, what God in his kindness has done through the churches in Macedonia. [2] They are being tested by many troubles, and they are very poor. But they are also filled with abundant joy, which has overflowed in rich generosity. [3] For I can testify that they gave not only what they could afford, but far more. And they did it of their own free will. [4] They begged us again and again for the privilege of sharing.
>
> 2 Corinthians 8:1–4 NLT

● What stands out to you the most about the generosity of these believers? Why?

- How often are you filled with "abundant joy" when giving to those in need? How would you describe your usual feelings after giving generously to someone who was in need?

- Have you ever begged someone for the privilege of giving to them or blessing them with your generosity? Why do you suppose these early believers considered giving such a privilege?

- How does giving generously, like these Macedonian Christians, reflect the kindness of God in action?

CHOOSING HOW YOU CHOOSE

Pre-deciding to be generous depends on planning as well as prompting. Planning keeps it practical and consistent. And responding to God's prompting becomes easier when you have a financial plan in place that's built on generosity. Once again, this may seem like a big ask, because we often have so many feelings and so much baggage attached to our views on money. But if you've struggled financially or haven't been following a budget consistently, then now is a great time to align your finances with your faith. And if your budget is already working for you and includes generosity, then it's a good time to review it for ways to give even more.

So log in to your bank accounts, open your apps, grab your checkbook, your cash envelopes, your file folders, whatever you've been using that indicates where your money goes—and conduct a generosity audit. Your goal is to identify what's been working well for you and your family in how you handle money and what needs some kind of adjustment, whether minor or major. Once you've reviewed the numbers and have a general sense of where you are, then it's time to look for ways to be more generous.

And it doesn't have to be giving more to your church, a local charity, or a global nonprofit. It could be partnering with your power company to pay a little extra to help others cover the cost of staying warm over the winter. It could be cleaning out your closets—or, if you want to get really generous, your garage—and donating as much as possible, anything and everything that's usable that no one in your household is using.

You might decide to go on an entertainment fast for a month—no online gaming, no new movies or streaming services, no books of any kind, no new music purchases. Then use what you would have normally spent on those items to help someone in need—a neighbor, a kid at your school, an elderly member of your church, a single parent, whoever has a need you have noticed. After you've completed your generosity audit and brainstormed ways to give more, reflect on the experience by answering the following questions.

- What was your biggest takeaway from reviewing your budget and conducting a generosity audit? What expense or ongoing expenditure surprised you?

- How could you immediately be more generous in giving to others?

- Who is someone you feel prompted to bless through a financial gift right now?

• Where can you cut back or tighten the budget in order to give above your tithe?

DETERMINING YOUR DECISIONS

Whether you relate more with the poor widow Jesus observed in the temple or billionaire philanthropist MacKenzie Scott, you know that generosity reflects who you are and how you choose to live. It's not a matter of how much you make, how much you have in savings, or how much you want to invest for retirement. How you give now reflects how you will give tomorrow and for the rest of your life—unless you choose to become more generous right now.

This is because if you want to be generous someday, you need to make today your someday. Decide today to be more generous. Whether you later have more or have less, whether you inherit millions from a long-lost relative or have to take on another job to make ends meet—regardless of your circumstances, you don't have to think about whether to be generous because you've already decided.

You were made in the image of a generous God who gave his Son for you. Your generous God says it's more blessed to give than receive. He knows you will be happier. You will better represent him. You will have more of an impact and leave a better legacy. You will be blessed because you were such a blessing to others.

The biggest change I'm making right away in order to be more generous is _____

_____

_____ .

No longer will I use the following excuses for reasons not to be generous: _____

_____

_____ .

Instead, I pre-decide to be generous right here and now because _____

_____

_____ .

PART 6

I WILL BE CONSISTENT

Deciding to be ready, devoted, faithful, influential, and generous won't have an impact unless you are consistent. It can be easy to know what you should do, but following through requires commitment to an ongoing process, not a one-time event. Consistency results from acting on your pre-decisions every day, doing what you have already decided to do. On a daily basis, the impact may seem small or hard to see, but over time consistency becomes cumulative. By pre-deciding that you will be consistent, you acknowledge the power of progress through continual practice. Here are the key principles you will learn in part 6:

- If you are going to stick to your pre-decisions, honor God, become everything you're meant to become, and live the life he has for you, then you must grow in your consistency.
- Without consistency, you are vulnerable to temptations, harmful addictions, destructive behavior, and the enemy's spiritual attacks.
- Successful people do consistently what other people do occasionally. Process precedes progress.
- If you want to grow in consistency, start with why. Shift from willpower to why-power.
- If you want to succeed, you need to plan to fail.
- If you fall in love with the process, you can win every day.
- Consistency requires community—people who support, encourage, pray, and help.
- Whatever it is, you can do it, with God's help.

THE POWER OF CONSISTENCY

*If your life is not what you want, it's likely because you've
been infected with inconsistency.*[36]

CRAIG GROESCHEL

Whether it's flossing and brushing, walking daily, or stretching each morning, the power of consistency has a huge impact on your health. So many of the habits related to establishing and sustaining physical and mental health require repetition and consistency. For instance, consider the booming industry focused on helping you lose weight. Millions of people buy the latest diet books, order special meals online, or rely only on one food group and often experience temporary results.

Many people who lose weight and keep it off, however, testify to a common-sense lifestyle approach for their success. They get in the habit of eating healthier food, more natural and less processed, exercise regularly by doing something sustainable, and pay attention to portions. What they do is important, but the impact comes from doing it regularly until it's part of their daily routine without thinking about it.

In his mega-bestselling book *Atomic Habits,* author James Clear reveals how he first learned the power of good habits in his life—recovering from a critical head injury that initially required a medically-induced coma for recovery. A high school baseball player, Clear got hit between the eyes full-force by a teammate's errant bat. Soon he recovered enough to be sent home but required many months of physical therapy to relearn basic skills.

"Between the seizures and my vision problems, it was eight months before I could drive a car again," Clear recalls. "At physical therapy, I practiced basic motor skills like walking in a straight line."[37] Eventually, Clear recovered fully and carried his new appreciation for the power of consistent habits with him into college. There, he became an outstanding student athlete, was named to the ESPN Academic All-America Team, and was awarded the President's Medal, his school's highest academic honor.

"We all deal with setbacks but in the long run, the quality of our lives often depends on the quality of our habits."[38]

- Do you agree the power of consistency is especially impactful on your health? What habits do you do consistently that have a cumulative positive effect?

- Have you ever had to recover from a major illness or injury like Clear experienced? If so, what role did consistency play in your recovery?

- On a scale of 1 to 10, with 1 being "impossible" and 10 being "quite easy," how challenging is it for you to start a new beneficial habit? Why that score?

- What's one health habit you wish you could begin and sustain? What would the impact of this habit be if you did it consistently for six months?

EXPLORING GOD'S WORD

It doesn't matter how many commitments you pre-decide if you don't follow through and do them consistently. Without the stick-to-itiveness of consistency, you may start all kinds of great habits and eliminate harmful ones temporarily. But for your pre-decisions to have the impact you desire, you have to keep doing them. And keep doing them.

Inconsistency has the power to kill your dreams, disrupt your life, and undermine your faith. The wisdom of Proverbs tell us, "A person without self-control is like a city with broken-down walls" (25:28 NLT). Without consistency, you remain vulnerable to temptations, powerful addictions, destructive behavior, and direct assaults from the enemy. Good intentions only pave roads to dead ends. If your life is not what you want, the problem may not be with your ability to make better decisions but with your inability to consistently act on them.

You may be familiar with the following passage in which Paul, writing to the believers in Rome, describes the push-pull craziness of doing what you know you don't want to do—and being unable to do what you know you want to do. As you read it this time, focus on what it reveals about the way inconsistency can wreck your peace of mind as well as your relationship with God.

15 I don't really understand myself, for I want to do what is right, but I don't do it. Instead, I do what I hate. 16 But if I know that what I am doing is wrong, this shows that I agree that the law is good. 17 So I am not the one doing wrong; it is sin living in me that does it.

18 And I know that nothing good lives in me, that is, in my sinful nature. I want to do what is right, but I can't. 19 I want to do what is good, but I don't. I don't want to do what is wrong, but I do it anyway. 20 But if I

do what I don't want to do, I am not really the one doing wrong; it is sin living in me that does it.

²¹ I have discovered this principle of life—that when I want to do what is right, I inevitably do what is wrong. ²² I love God's law with all my heart. ²³ But there is another power within me that is at war with my mind. This power makes me a slave to the sin that is still within me. ²⁴ Oh, what a miserable person I am! Who will free me from this life that is dominated by sin and death? ²⁵ Thank God! The answer is in Jesus Christ our Lord.

ROMANS 7:15–25 NLT

- Based on this passage, how would Paul define consistency? Why does he say we're unable to be as consistent as we want based on our own power?

- How does the power of Christ enable you to be consistent in obeying God and living constructively? How does living in your own power keep you stuck in inconsistency?

- When have you recently felt the internal turmoil and emotional conflict Paul describes here? What was the catalyst sending you into this mindset?

- What impact has inconsistency had on your life up until now?

EMBRACING THE TRUTH

Rather than trying to make a lot of big changes at once, you will likely have greater success if you start with small habits and build upon them. As you begin to see the positive effects of implementing one habit, you become motivated to add another and create momentum. By pre-deciding to be consistent, you also make two other choices: to honor your other commitments to God and to rely on his power to do what you cannot do on your own.

We see this kind of progressive consistency in the life of Daniel in the Old Testament. As a captive taken from his home in Israel and forced to live in the pagan culture of Babylon, Daniel would have been justified in feeling powerless over his circumstances. After all, no amount of individual willpower could overthrow the vast armies of his captors. Yet Daniel did what he had always done—relied on God and maintained his integrity.

Whether refusing the king's rich food and wine or maintaining his daily prayer times, Daniel chose to remain consistent in doing what he knew to do. The impact of his consistency extended far beyond his own life and made a transformative difference on countless generations.

> [3] Daniel soon proved himself more capable than all the other administrators and high officers. Because of Daniel's great ability, the king made plans to place him over the entire empire. [4] Then the other administrators and high officers began searching for some fault in the way Daniel was handling government affairs, but they couldn't find anything to criticize or condemn. He was faithful, always responsible, and completely trustworthy.
>
> DANIEL 6:3–4 NLT

- When have you justified not being consistent with constructive habits because of painful or unexpected circumstances? What contributed to your habits deteriorating?

- When have you found that remaining consistent with good habits helped you endure a trial, overcome a temptation, or withstand the enemy's assault?

- What did Daniel reveal about God's character by remaining consistent in his faith? How would you describe the impact that Daniel's consistency had on his Babylonian captors?

- What potential impact could your consistency have on your family, your friends, your coworkers, and future generations? What needs to happen for you to cultivate more consistency in your life?

CHOOSING HOW YOU CHOOSE

As you have likely experienced, good intentions lack the staying power of committed consistency. If you rely on your feelings or circumstances to reinforce your consistency, then it likely won't happen. Rather than relying on willpower or self-discipline to remain consistent, it helps to remain mindful of why you want to do what you're doing consistently.

For example, why did Daniel, a prisoner of war held captive in a foreign culture, continue to pray consistently? Because he was devoted to God and knew that connecting with God through prayer three times each day reflected his devotion and maintained his connection to the Lord. He was focused on his purpose, which in turn fueled his plan.

Daniel, along with countless other consistent men and women, knew that if you're not clear on why you're doing something, what you're doing isn't enough. If you haven't defined the purpose of doing what you want to become a habit, then you will soon get tired, distracted, or overwhelmed by life's demands. You need to start with your why and allow it to drive your what.

With this goal in mind, consider three positive habits you want to start or have started but struggle to sustain. Using the space below, identify your why for each one and then describe how this why can motivate you to be consistent in doing these habits.

HABIT 1

Your **what**	Your **why**

HABIT 2

Your **what**	Your **why**

HABIT 3

Your **what**	Your **why**

DETERMINING YOUR DECISIONS

Shifting from willpower to why-power won't guarantee consistency—but it will increase the likelihood of focusing on your motive and desired outcome. The big problem, of course, is that willpower fades over time and gets depleted by the interruptions, distractions, and hectic pace of a busy life. So when your decisions meet resistance—and you will always experience resistance—then you can't keep doing what you're committed to doing.

Which is why pre-deciding to focus on why-power also allows you to focus on God's power. Knowing your why can make all the difference. In the face of temptation, trials, tension, and turmoil, a strong why pushes through excuses and overcomes detractors. You know why you're doing what you're doing no matter how you feel, what the weather's like, or how much work you need to do. You have pre-decided to be consistent in maintaining holy habits, and with God's help, you can.

As you reflect and identify your why for being consistent, you often need to dig deep in order to find your most powerful motivator. Avoiding conflict might be a why, but not one that's strong enough to support your goal of loving your spouse wholeheartedly. Instead, consider the benefits of honest, open communication—including when you disagree with one another. Looking attractive might be a why for losing weight, but experiencing the benefits of lower blood pressure when dealing with stress might have greater power to motivate.

So review your whys for the three habits you listed above. Do you need to revise them in order to go deeper? Spend a few moments in prayer, asking the Holy Spirit to guide you, and then see if you can identify better, richer reasons that will motivate you for the long haul.

PLAN TO FAIL AND LOVE THE PROCESS

What holds us back isn't perfection but the illusion of perfection.[39]

CRAIG GROESCHEL

Scientists and inventors are notorious fail-ers. Not failures—but fail-ers. Because the best scientists and most successful inventors embrace failure as being one step closer to their next insight, a new discovery, an innovative approach. Thomas Edison not only failed school before going on to become an iconic inventor, but according to his records, he failed 2,774 times before achieving a satisfactory design of an electric light bulb.[40] Apparently, failure allowed Edison to adjust his plan and process in order to come one step closer to his goal.

Madame Marie Curie, famed as a pioneering physicist exploring radioactivity, persevered through the trial-and-error failures of research yet struggled with personal heartbreak. In the wake of being the first woman to be awarded the Nobel Prize in physics, along with her husband, Pierre, and another scientist in 1903, Marie Curie battled the prejudice of a male-dominated field.

Three years later, her beloved husband and research partner died in a train accident. Madame Curie continued her work but was overtly rejected for membership in the prestigious French Academy of Sciences in 1911. That same year, however, Curie was singularly awarded the Nobel Prize a second time in the field of chemistry in recognition of her studies on radium and polonium. She remains the only woman to receive the Nobel twice for two different fields of study.[41]

A few years after Curie's second Nobel, another physicist and Nobel Prize-winner, Niels Bohr, extended the understanding of radiation through his research on atomic structure. He viewed failure as crucial and essential to his scientific process. "An expert," Bohr said, "is a person who has made all the mistakes that can be made in a very narrow field."[42]

Embracing failure and allowing it to help you adjust your plan is not just for scientists and inventors. If you're committed to being consistent, then you learn to love the process—including failure.

- Have you ever pursued a goal or built or created something in which you viewed failure as necessary for your end result? Or do you usually view failure as an obstacle or sign of imperfection?

- What resonates with you when you consider the way people like Edison, Curie, and Bohr embraced failure and persevered to achieve their remarkable goals?

- When was a recent time you considered something you attempted a failure? What caused you to fail?

- How has your perception of failure hindered your ability to be consistent in cultivating good habits?

EXPLORING GOD'S WORD

Rather than planning to fail and learning from the process, you may get stuck in pursuing perfection. Without a doubt, perfectionism blocks the path to making great decisions. Too often, you put yourself in an all-or-nothing mindset that prevents you from even trying. You assume, "If I can't do this perfectly—and keep doing it perfectly—then why bother?" Like so many other deceptions of the enemy, perfection becomes an unattainable condition for persistence and consistency.

But perfection is an illusion.

We assume that because God is perfect in every way, we must somehow please him through our attempts to be exactly like him. Two problems with this assumption. First, God's perfection is dynamic and powerful, holy and transformative. Perfection from a human perspective tends to be a static state of harmonious equilibrium, a moral purity that's free from sin. Perfection from God's point of view reflects his goodness, his love, and his grace.

Second, we are only made perfect—whole and holy—through the power of Christ's death on the cross and the free gift of salvation. Our sinful tendencies linger in various ways in this life but do not define who we are. When we accept God's grace and live for him, we become co-heirs with Jesus, a child of the King of kings. As we mature in our faith and become more like Christ, we reflect God's mercy and love—not an ideal state of morality that amounts to legalism.

You're never going to be perfect, but you can be consistent.

The key? Relying on grace day by day and falling in love with the process of becoming more like Jesus. Focusing on results is the downfall of people who want to be consistent. If you fall in love with the process, you can win every day.

[14] So then, since we have a great High Priest who has entered heaven, Jesus the Son of God, let us hold firmly to what we believe. [15] This High Priest of ours understands our weaknesses, for he faced all of the same testings we do, yet he did not sin. [16] So let us come boldly to the throne of our gracious God. There we will receive his mercy, and we will find grace to help us when we need it most.

HEBREWS 4:14–16 NLT

- What difference does it make knowing that Jesus understands your weaknesses, struggles, and failures? That he faced all the same testings that you do?

- How does recognizing the way Jesus suffered and triumphed inspire you to hold firmly to what you believe? To persevere in being consistent?

- How does God's grace allow you to learn from your mistakes and failures? How does his grace alter your pursuit of perfectionism?

- How does coming boldly to your gracious God and receiving his mercy help you when you're tempted to stumble?

EMBRACING THE TRUTH

Consistency builds when you just do what you need to do today.

And then do it the next day. And the next.

You must remember that consistency is not a single event or a one-time decision—it's an ongoing process. The more you grow in being consistent, the more you experience momentum to keep going. The keys to consistency include focusing on your why, not your what; planning to fail and learning from your failures; and falling in love with the process of persevering.

Consistency also requires community.

You simply can't be consistent on your own—no one can. But you are not on your own. You're never alone when you rely on God's power to keep going and connect with other people traveling in your same direction. Brothers and sisters in your faith family are especially vital to maintaining consistency. They provide prayer, encouragement, trust, support, and accountability. They remind you of what's true and eternal when you're blinded by what's deceptive and temporary.

So if you want to pre-decide to be consistent, you must be intentional about forming your team for support. You can't be consistent without them. You need them—and they need you—to cheer you on and hold you accountable for doing what you've committed to do consistently. Helping one other grow in the faith, including the decisions you make on a daily basis, isn't a luxury or something nice if you happen to have it. Community is essential for consistency.

[9] Two people are better off than one, for they can help each other succeed. [10] If one person falls, the other can reach out and help. But someone who falls alone is in real trouble. [11] Likewise, two people lying close

together can keep each other warm. But how can one be warm alone? [12] A person standing alone can be attacked and defeated, but two can stand back-to-back and conquer. Three are even better, for a triple-braided cord is not easily broken.

ECCLESIASTES 4:9–12 NLT

- According to this passage, what are the benefits of relationships with others in helping one another succeed? When have you experienced this in your life?

- Does it come naturally for you to connect with others for support when trying to add good habits or eliminate bad ones? Why do you suppose you're this way?

- When has someone recently encouraged you, prayed with you, or simply listened to you in a way that helped you persevere and keep going? Was your interaction unplanned, or do you regularly connect and check in with this person?

- How has God used you in someone else's life to encourage, support, and help them keep going when they were facing challenges? How did helping them encourage you to be more consistent?

CHOOSING HOW YOU CHOOSE

Like most people, you probably try to avoid failure as much as possible. After all, who wants to fail? You want to resist temptation, be faithful to God, and reflect his love to everyone around you. In other words, you want to avoid failure by being perfect. But as you know, this is never going to work.

If you're obsessed with achieving your goal, you will likely grow impatient and feel like progress is taking forever. If you are focused on your win, every day you still haven't achieved it might feel like you're losing. And if you're losing, then why keep trying, right?

But if you fall in love with the process, you can win every day.

Remember, it often takes time before you see the results of consistency. You do the right thing for a few weeks or months, but you may still feel out of shape or in too much debt or without the intimate connection you want to enjoy with your spouse. It's okay to acknowledge those feelings, but you must redefine success.

Because success is not when you hit the goal in the future.

You're successful—and being consistent—when you do what you need to do today. This means that daily success and ongoing consistency require a process. And your process will always precede your progress.

If you can fall in love with that process, the results will follow. And as you work your plan and see some progress, you will *want* to do it consistently every day. And if you do it consistently, you *will* reach your goal. If, instead, you fall in love with the goal, every day you don't achieve your goal, you will feel like a failure. Eventually, you'll get frustrated and quit, never reaching your desired result.

Consistency requires loving the process—not perfection.

- On a scale of 1 to 10, with 1 being "never or rarely" and 10 being "always and daily," how often are you aware of perfectionistic tendencies in yourself? How have you usually coped with perfectionism in your life?

- Based on reading part 6 in *Think Ahead* as well as your own experience, what does it mean for you to plan to fail? How can this reinforce your commitment to consistency?

- Similarly, what does it look like for you to focus on the process as progress rather than fixating on future success?

- What's your greatest challenge with embracing the process and focusing on what you need to do for today? Impatience, busyness, frustration, shame, lack of support? Something else?

DETERMINING YOUR DECISIONS

We often refer to "moral support" as a way of helping others by being with them emotionally and psychologically. But the term also aptly describes the way other people can help us maintain the beliefs and values informing our faith—and our decisions. The moral support of key people is essential when implementing our pre-decision to be someone who is consistent.

Depending on your personality, relational style, emotional state, circumstances, and other variables, you may or may not feel comfortable seeking others for the support you need to be consistent. Gender dynamics can also factor in to your willingness to ask for help, depending on how you were conditioned and what you learned growing up about how women relate to one another and how men relate to one another.

Generally, women may enjoy more freedom in pursuing close friendships and asking for help from other women. Men, on the other hand, may struggle to go below surface topics with other men because they believe men should be strong and independent and not need anyone's help. Sometimes there's also a power dynamic or competitive vibe among men that makes it more challenging to be vulnerable and ask for support.

Regardless, everyone needs a team, a group, a tribe to help them be consistent so they can grow in their faith and make the best decisions possible. With this goal in mind, think through the following questions and the next steps required for you to be intentional about getting the support you need to succeed.

- Do you agree that having the support of other people is essential for being consistent? Why or why not?

- How difficult is it for you to be authentic with others and let them know your honest struggles and real-life challenges? What tends to prevent you from being more vulnerable and connecting with trusted friends at a deeper level?

- Who are the people right now who support you emotionally, psychologically, and spiritually? How have you experienced their support in the past month?

- What or who are you lacking in your support team right now? Who can you ask to help provide what you need in order to fulfill your commitment to consistency?

I WILL BE A FINISHER

Pre-deciding that you will never quit ensures that you persevere even when you don't feel like it or circumstances are tough. When you commit not to quit, you trust that God's power, provision, purpose, and peace will be more than sufficient for you. You may not see how you can get where he's calling you to go, but you trust him enough to take the next step and then the next, day by day. By pre-deciding that you will be a finisher, you commit to following through on all the pre-decisions you've made. Here are the key principles you will learn in part 7:

- If you're not dead, you're not done. God has more for you.
- Every time you are strong in the Lord and persevere, you cast a vote that you will be a finisher. When you commit, you do not quit.
- Successful people succeed because of grit—not necessarily because of talent, connections, training, or education.
- You can overcome, achieve your goals, and live an amazing, God-honoring life if you just keep putting one foot in front of the other.
- You will be tempted to quit because you can't see the future. But you don't have to finish the race today. You just need to take one more step.
- When you fix your eyes on Jesus, you put your confidence in God instead of in yourself.
- When you fix your eyes on Jesus, you have confidence because you can do all things through his strength, and your confidence will be rewarded.

VOTING ON YOUR FUTURE

Today's decisions are votes on what kind of person you will be tomorrow. . . . Every time you are strong in the Lord and persevere, you cast a vote that you will be a finisher.[43]

CRAIG GROESCHEL

The term "bucket list" became popular again thanks to the 2007 film by the same name starring Jack Nicholson and Morgan Freeman. They portray two terminally ill men who decide to fulfill their list of goals and destinations before they "kick the bucket," thus explaining why they call it their bucket list. As the term's usage has grown in popularity, so has compiling and completing a list of experiences, events, and extraordinary places one wants to check off the list before dying.

Many people, often those entering what they perceive to be the second half of their lives, keep written lists describing the remaining goals they hope to accomplish before they die. Some goals are doable while others may seem more unlikely or improbable. But keeping a bucket list begins the process of naming something important to them, something in some way significant and worth pursuing. For the characters in the film, a bucket list provides focus and incentive to help them make the most of their remaining time alive and enjoy a quality of life they have previously been too busy to pursue.

Whether you have a bucket list or not, you have a choice about how you live the rest of your life and what you accomplish. You can continue doing what you're doing and living like you're living. Or, you can commit that you will never quit.

- Do you keep a bucket list of things you want to do and places you want to visit before you die? How many items have you checked off your bucket list?

- What's one bucket list item you are already planning to pursue? Why does it appeal to you as something you want to do before you die?

- Do you tend to be someone who finishes most things they start? Or have you generally struggled to follow through and complete what you began?

- Considering your present age and stage of life, what does it mean for you to finish strong? What does it mean for you to commit to being a finisher?

EXPLORING GOD'S WORD

Most people have at least a few decisions they regret in their lives. Perhaps you have regrets about things you've quit on in the past or struggle to complete right now. You wish you could be more willing to finish what you start, but you struggle to know how to do this. Like our other pre-decisions, however, before you focus on your how, you must focus on your why.

Whether or not you decide to be a finisher determines the kind of person you are and how you will live the rest of your life. Basically, every decision you make is a vote on your future. Today's decisions are votes on what kind of person you will be tomorrow. Any time you quit, you vote on becoming a person who doesn't have what it takes and doesn't finish what they started.

But every time you are strong in the Lord and choose to persevere, you cast a vote that you will be a finisher.

5 But you should keep a clear mind in every situation. Don't be afraid of suffering for the Lord. Work at telling others the Good News, and fully carry out the ministry God has given you. 6 As for me, my life has already been poured out as an offering to God. The time of my death is near. 7 I have fought the good fight, I have finished the race, and I have remained faithful. 8 And now the prize awaits me—the crown of righteousness, which the Lord, the righteous Judge, will give me on the day of his return.

2 TIMOTHY 4:5–8 NLT

● Why do you suppose Paul emphasized keeping a clear mind in every situation? How does keeping a clear mind relate to a fear of suffering?

- What does Paul's valediction to his protégé Timothy reveal about what it means to finish well? What's required to fight the good fight and finish the race of faith?

- What word or phrase here speaks to your heart or resonates with what you need to commit to finishing well?

- What does it mean for your life to be poured out as an offering to God? How does pre-deciding that you will never quit honor God and what he has called you to do?

EMBRACING THE TRUTH

Facing his imminent death, Paul shared his final words of wisdom in his letters to the man he had mentored and trained in sharing the gospel, Timothy. Paul made it clear that he was finishing his life with peace because he had been faithful in completing his commitments to honor God in all that he did. Without boasting in his own efforts, Paul celebrated the way God had allowed him to do all that he pre-decided to do after dramatically encountering Christ while on the road to Damascus.

Years earlier, he had written about the pre-decision he had made: "I consider my life worth nothing to me; my only aim is to finish the race and complete the task the Lord Jesus has given me—the task of testifying to the good news of God's grace" (Acts 20:24). Now at the end of his race, Paul tells Timothy, "I did it. I did what God gave me to do. I am a finisher."

Paul encourages us in the same way he encouraged Timothy. Yes, you will face difficult times. Unexpected losses and devastating disappointments will likely occur. You will suffer along the way and may feel like giving up. But no matter what, you must never give up. You are a finisher. When you commit, you don't quit: "So let's not get tired of doing what is good. At just the right time we will reap a harvest of blessing if we don't give up" (Galatians 6:9 NLT).

- Why do you suppose Paul said that he considered his life worth nothing to him? What was Paul's basis for considering his life valuable?

- What do you want to be able to say with confidence when you are at the end of your life? What would you pass on to the next generation of believers?

- When have you been tempted to quit something recently—a relationship, job, project, goal? Do you regret quitting, or was it a necessary, constructive choice?

- What are you suffering right now that makes it hard for you to keep going in your faith? In your daily life?

CHOOSING HOW YOU CHOOSE

Paul went from being a relentless persecutor of Christians—basically a zealous bounty hunter capable of violence—to one of the most impactful followers of Jesus who ever lived. After his encounter with Jesus, Paul created a kind of spiritual bucket list—places he wanted to visit in order to spread the good news of Christ, fellow believers he wanted to mentor, letters he wished to write in order to instruct, advise, and encourage. He fulfilled all of those objectives and more.

But they didn't happen accidentally. Once he was a believer, Paul pre-decided that he would finish the good work God had started in him. Without hesitation, he was all in when it came to pursuing the Lord and telling others about Jesus. Because of his faithfulness, Paul could then celebrate the impact his life had and use his remaining time to write and encourage Timothy.

When you consider the life of Paul, or any of the giants of the Christian faith, you may be tempted to view them as incomparable—people of faith who did things that you could never do. But with all due respect to their accomplishments and the amazing lives they led to the end, the saints of God relied on his power to do what they knew they could not do themselves. They simply trusted him and remained consistent in their obedience. They followed God's guidance and plugged into the power of the Holy Spirit.

You have access to the same Spirit of God who empowered Paul and every other believer. What will determine the difference between the impact your life will have and their spiritual legacy is what you decide right now. The goals you set and pursue today determine the impact your faith will have on those around you—now as well as later.

- Think for a moment about what your spiritual bucket list might look like. What goals would you put on your faith bucket list? Why?

- When you think about the kind of prayer warrior and intercessor you want to be, what can you put on your bucket list to do consistently in order to be that person of prayer?

- What about your relationship with God's Word? What bucket list goal do you want to set for yourself that will keep you engaged and actively learning and growing in the Word?

- Where do you want to go in order to stretch your faith? A missions trip? Seminary? Your small group retreat?

DETERMINING YOUR DECISIONS

Professional athletes, coaches, and sports psychologists rely on visualization as a key tool for improving performance. Through a variety of methods, they focus on who they want to become, the games they want to win, the kind of team they want to be part of, and the impact they can have both on and off the playing field. From those goals, they work backward to think about what's required to make that vision come to life. Then they dedicate themselves to the process and commit to fulfilling their potential.

If you want to be a finisher, the vision you have for yourself is just as important as that of any Olympic medalist or pro player. Knowing what you care about most, knowing how God has made you, knowing where you are in your life—what do you want to make sure you finish? Who will you be at this time next year? How will you be closer to God and more mature in your faith? Those won't happen by accident but by pre-deciding now to finish becoming all that God has made you to be.

At some prior time you may have completed an exercise in which you write your own eulogy or consider the kind of legacy you want to leave. Now is a good time to revisit where you want to finish and how you will live to get there. It doesn't need to be larger than life or what others expect—only who you believe God created you to be and what he has called you to do. Whatever you want to call it—your eulogy, spiritual legacy statement, or personal visualization, use the space below to write a paragraph describing how your life looks now that you are pre-deciding to finish strong.

TAKE ANOTHER STEP

*When God calls you, when you know it's important,
you don't quit. It's not an option.*[44]

CRAIG GROESCHEL

S ometimes a marathon is about a finishing time, and sometimes it's about making it to the start."[45] In an online article for *Runner's World*, Jennifer Van Allen expressed her struggle with pressuring herself to beat her personal record each time she runs a marathon. It's the plight of many longtime runners who are always looking for ways to improve and go faster.

But then she realized that her circumstances differed from race to race. When she realized all the challenges she faced—nursing a newborn, commuting daily for work, sleeping only a few hours a night, she was able to readjust her perspective.

She concluded, "I want the marathon to be about the finishing time. I want to carve a fitter, faster version of myself out of the current model. But the only way I can get there is by acknowledging and starting where I am. All I can do is take it one step at a time."[46]

Choosing to be a finisher works the same way. You have to start where you are. Stop comparing yourself to whatever perfect standard you may hold. Embrace the process. And keep taking one step after another—until you have run your race.

- Can you relate to this runner's struggle to improve her time for each race she completed? What's something you're always trying to improve or do better?

- When you consider where you are right now, what's one change in your life that can help you pre-decide to be a finisher?

- What's required for you to persevere and continue running the race of faith? What does it mean for you to pre-decide that no matter what, you won't quit?

- When you're struggling and discouraged enough to stop doing what you know you want to do, what reminds you to keep going? How can you realize that staying in the race is actually winning?

EXPLORING GOD'S WORD

You will likely continue to struggle at times in your life—but never let your struggle become your quit. When you commit, you no longer have to consider whether you will finish—because you know you will not quit. Others may see you struggle or hit an obstacle and stumble momentarily. Some may even advise you to quit, to step away, to let it go. But your commitment to God not to quit determines what you will do in those most challenging, painful moments.

Perseverance is your path to greatness.

Just as it's easy to sprint at the beginning of a race and run on nervous energy and adrenaline, it's just as easy to get excited and feel enthusiastic about something at the beginning of a new endeavor. But then the excitement wears off and the tedious, uncomfortable reality sets in. You're no longer enthusiastic—you're weary. Nevertheless, you just keep putting one foot in front of the other, walking by faith another hour, another day. This is endurance. This is what it means to be a finisher.

And you know you can do it because you have grit.

Grit keeps your eyes focused on Jesus.

Grit reminds you that his power is in you.

You can do all things through Christ who strengthens you.

[1] Let us throw off everything that hinders and the sin that so easily entangles. And let us run with perseverance the race marked out for us, [2] fixing our eyes on Jesus, the pioneer and perfecter of faith. For the joy set before him he endured the cross, scorning its shame, and sat down at the right hand of the throne of God.

HEBREWS 12:1-2

- How would you describe grit? What does it look like in your own life?

- Do you agree that grit is essential to run the race of faith? Why or why not?

- What are some ways you can keep your eyes fixed on Jesus when you want to quit? How can his example empower you to keep going?

- What is the joy set before you in the race you're running right now? How does this joy overcome shame and help you to persevere?

EMBRACING THE TRUTH

Grit relies on grace.

You may not be the most talented or most capable, the best educated or most experienced. You might not know the right people or have the right connections. Your success does not rely on any of those, though. Your grit gets you through. You can overcome, achieve your goals, and live an amazing, God-honoring life if you just keep putting one foot in front of the other.

Sure, you will be tempted to quit at times. Your circumstances will change. Some relationships may drift apart while others surprise you with their betrayal. You may experience a health crisis, an injury, or a disease that feels like it changes your commitment to quit. But deep down, you know that nothing can change your grit when you've committed not to quit.

You may grow weary, but you don't have to finish the race today.

You just need to take one more step.

- When have you relied on something other than grit and grace to keep you going? How did that turn out?

- What can you do to recharge and replenish your faith when you begin feeling weary and overwhelmed by life? What has helped you rest in the past?

- What major obstacles have you already faced to get to where you are now? How did you push through them?

- Prior to reading *Think Ahead* and completing this workbook, what motivated you to persevere in your faith? What motivates you now?

CHOOSING HOW YOU CHOOSE

When you fix your eyes on Jesus, you have confidence because you know you can do all things through his strength and that your confidence will be rewarded. From the beginning, Jesus had pre-decided, "I am ready, devoted, an influencer, faithful, generous, consistent, and when I commit, I don't quit, because I am a finisher." He set the example for you so you can know how to persevere by relying on his power.

He was *ready*.

Jesus faced all the temptations you face, yet he never sinned. That's why he was able to go to the cross and take on your sins as an innocent sacrifice.

He was *devoted*.

God was so devoted to you he sent his Son, and Jesus died for you.

He was *faithful*.

He has promised to be faithful to us because of who he is: "If we are faithless, he remains faithful, for he cannot disown himself" (2 Timothy 2:13).

He was an *influencer*.

Jesus remains the most influential person who ever lived, changing all of history forever. You wouldn't be reading this or considering how to follow his example otherwise.

He was *generous*.

God is so giving that he gave his one and only Son to die for you. Your generosity reflects his character because you are made in his image.

He was *consistent*.

He is "the same yesterday and today and forever" (Hebrews 13:8). His absolute consistency allows you to fully trust him in every moment, and now you want to live with that same consistency so you can become more trustworthy too.

He was a *finisher*.

Before the creation of the world, the holy Trinity (God the Father, God the Son, and God the Holy Spirit) planned how to save you and all people. That pre-decision led Jesus to strip himself of the glory of heaven and come to earth and to die for you. He was tempted to opt out of the plan, but refused, going to the cross, from which he declared, "It is finished" (John 19:30).

- How does Jesus' ability to finish what he pre-decided empower you to follow his example?

- Which of these seven pre-decisions remains the most difficult for you? Why do you think this is the case?

- Which of these seven pre-decisions do you feel most confident about right now? What is the source of your confidence?

- The next time you're struggling, weary, or feel like giving up, what's one thing you will remember to keep you going? How will this help you persevere?

DETERMINING YOUR DECISIONS

Now that you have completed this workbook, your next steps will determine the impact of your pre-decisions. You've read and reflected, studied and prayed, and now it's time to own all that you've absorbed and apply it in action. Your commitment to these seven pre-decisions means nothing if you're not willing to persevere and finish what you've started.

To remind you of all you've learned, look back through your responses, notes, and completed exercises in the previous pages. Go back and look through *Think Ahead* and what you underlined, highlighted, and tagged to remember. Standing from your new vantage point, answer the following questions as you evaluate your experience and take your next steps—one after another. And then the next.

- What stood out as you looked through your past responses and exercises? What consistent themes or threads seemed to emerge?

- How has your relationship with God changed over the course of reading *Think Ahead* and completing this workbook? What evidence do you already see of this change in the ways you think, speak, and act?

- What has surprised you most over the course of this study? What do you understand more fully now that you didn't prior to completing this workbook journey?

- What's your big takeaway from the process of making these seven pre-decisions? What will ensure your ability to fight the good fight and finish your race?

CONCLUSION

You will recall from reading *Think Ahead* that on average, you face 35,000 decisions on an typical day. In the pages of this workbook, you have focused on drastically reducing that overwhelming number by pre-deciding to commit to seven essential qualities that will automatize many of those thousands of choices and fuel you on a path to the abundant life Jesus offers.

You don't have to continue making those 35,000 decisions the same way, the way that's caused you to get to where you are right now. If you want more of what you have, then you can keep doing more of what you already do. If you want the same life you've been living, then continue living the same old way. If you've completed this workbook, however, you likely want so much more, a new way, something better.

You're sick and tired of losing battles to the devil, giving in to temptation, and regretting sinning against God.

You're done living with good spiritual intentions but not following through.

You sense deep down that God has more for you. That he doesn't just want you to be happy or successful, but faithful.

You hate being easily influenced by the people and patterns of this world. You're ready to be salt and light, influencing others toward Jesus each day.

You're fed up with being selfish and now long to live with a heart of incredible generosity.

You're weary from being inconsistent, but driven by why-power, you're now ready to do consistently what you used to do occasionally.

You're ready to draw a line in the sand that says when you commit, you don't quit.

You have decided it's time to stop reacting and start thinking ahead. It's time to make seven pre-decisions that will change your life:

1. You will be ready.
2. You will be devoted.
3. You will be faithful.
4. You will be an influencer.
5. You will be generous.
6. You will be consistent.
7. You will be a finisher.

You have pre-decided to honor God in the most important areas of your life. So get ready—because you are ready to think ahead and never look back!

LEADER'S GUIDE

This workbook is a companion to *Think Ahead*, and it's designed for both individuals and groups. If you're participating in a group study that has designated you as its leader, thank you for agreeing to serve in this capacity. What you have chosen to do is valuable and will make a great difference in the lives of others.

Think Ahead is a fifteen-lesson study built around individual completion of this workbook and small-group interaction. As the group leader, just think of yourself as the host of a dinner party. Your job is to take care of your guests by managing all the behind-the-scenes details so that when everyone arrives, they can just enjoy time together.

As group leader, your role is not to answer all the questions or reteach the content—the book, this workbook, and the Holy Spirit will do most of that work. Your job is to guide the experience and create an environment where people can process, question, and reflect—not receive more instruction.

Make sure everyone in the group gets a copy of the workbook. This will keep everyone on the same page and help the process run more smoothly. If some group members are unable to purchase the workbook, arrange it so that people can share the resource with other group members. Everyone should feel free to write in their workbooks and bring them to group every week.

SETTING UP THE GROUP

As the group leader, you'll want to create an environment that encourages sharing and learning. A church sanctuary or formal classroom may not be as ideal as a living room because those locations can feel formal and less intimate. No matter what setting you choose, provide enough comfortable seating for everyone, and, if possible, arrange the seats in a semicircle so everyone can share more easily. This will make group interaction and conversation more efficient and natural.

Try to get to the meeting site early so you can greet participants as they arrive. Simple refreshments create a welcoming atmosphere and can be a wonderful addition to a group study evening. Try to take food and pet allergies into account to make your guests as comfortable as possible. You may also want to consider offering childcare to those with children who want to attend. Managing these details up front will make the rest of your group experience flow smoothly and provide a welcoming space in which to engage with the content of *Think Ahead*.

STARTING YOUR GROUP TIME

Once everyone has arrived, it's time to begin the group. Here are some simple tips to make your group time healthy, enjoyable, and effective.

First, begin the meeting with a short prayer, and remind the group members to put their phones on silent. This is a way to make sure you can all be present with one another and with God. Then, give each person one or two minutes to check in before diving into the material. In your first session, participants can introduce themselves and share what they hope to experience in this group study. Beginning with your second session, people may need more time to share their insights from their personal studies and enjoy getting better acquainted.

As you begin going through the material, invite members to share their experiences and discuss their responses. Usually, you won't answer the discussion questions yourself, but you may need to go first a couple of times to set an example, answering briefly and with a reasonable amount of transparency. You may also want to help participants process what they're learning as they complete each session ahead of each group meeting. Debriefing like this is a bit different from responding to questions about the material because the content comes from their real lives. The basic experiences that you want the group to reflect on are:

- *What was the best part about this week's lesson?*
- *What was the hardest part?*
- *What did I learn about myself?*
- *What did I learn about God?*

LEADING THE DISCUSSION TIME

Encourage all the group members to participate in the discussion, but make sure they know they don't have to do so. As the discussion progresses, you may want to follow up with comments such as, "Tell me more about that," or, "Why did you answer that way?" This will allow the group participants to deepen their reflections as you invite meaningful sharing in a nonthreatening way.

While each session in this workbook includes multiple sections, you do not have to go through each section and cover every question or exercise. Feel free to go with the dynamic in the group and skip around if needed to cover all the material more naturally. You can pick and choose questions based on either the needs of your group or how the conversation is flowing. Also, don't be afraid of silence. Offering a question and allowing up to thirty seconds of silence is okay. It allows people space to think about how they want to respond and also gives them time to do so.

As group leader, you are the boundary keeper for your group. Do not let anyone (yourself included) dominate the group time. Keep an eye out for group members who might be tempted to "attack" folks they disagree with or try to "fix" those having struggles. These kinds of behaviors can derail a group's momentum, so they need to be steered in a different direction. Model active listening and encourage everyone in your group to do the same. This will make your group time a safe space and create a positive community.

At the end of each group session, encourage the participants to take just a few minutes to review what they've learned and write down one or two key takeaways. This will help them cement the big ideas in their minds as you close the session. Close your time together with prayer as a group.

Remember to have fun. Spending time with others and growing closer to God is a gift to enjoy and embrace. And get ready for God to change your thinking and change your life.

Thank you again for taking the time to lead your group. You are making a difference in the lives of others and having an impact on the kingdom of God.

ENDNOTES

1. Craig Groeschel, *Think Ahead* (Grand Rapids, MI: Zondervan, 2024), 28.
2. "Here's How 15 Women Lost 50+ Pounds," Health.com, https://www.health.com/weight-loss/weight-loss-success-stories-before-after.
3. Ibid.
4. Groeschel, *Think Ahead*, 38.
5. Abby Tang and Michelle Yan Huang, "Airplane Accidents Are 95% Survivable," Business Insider, February 4, 2020, https://www.businessinsider.com/seven-ways-increase-your-odds-surviving-plane-crash-2020-1.
6. Ibid.
7. Groeschel, *Think Ahead*, 49.
8. Mandalit del Barco, "'King Richard,' the Oscar-nominated Film, Authentically Depicts the Williams' History," NPR, https://www.npr.org/2022/03/16/1086682631/king-richard-the-oscar-nominated-film-authentically-depicts-the-williams-history.
9. Ibid.
10. Groeschel, *Think Ahead*, 57.
11. Katherine Dillinger, "Surgeon General Lays Out Framework to Tackle Loneliness and 'Mend the Social Fabric of Our Nation,'" CNN, May 2, 2023, https://www.cnn.com/2023/05/02/health/murthy-loneliness-isolation/index.html.
12. "Loneliness Minister: 'It's More Important Than Ever to Take Action," GOV.UK, June 17, 2021, https://www.gov.uk/government/news/loneliness-minister-its-more-important-than-ever-to-take-action.
13. Dillinger, "Surgeon General Lays Out Framework to Tackle Loneliness and 'Mend the Social Fabric of Our Nation.'"
14. Groeschel, *Think Ahead*, 85.
15. Lori Keong, "Joanna Gaines Transforms Three Rooms with Speedy, Cost-Effective DIY Ideas," January 31, 2023, https://www.architecturaldigest.com/story/joanna-gaines-debuts-a-mini-reni-series.
16. Ibid.
17. Groeschel, *Think Ahead*, 94.
18. Richard Pallardy, "2010 Haiti Earthquake," Britannica, August 9, 2023, https://www.britannica.com/event/2010-Haiti-earthquake.
19. David Vanderpool, MD, *Live Beyond* (Nashville, TN: Forefront Books, 2020), 16–17.
20. Groeschel, *Think Ahead*, 98.
21. Tom Huddleston Jr, "This Top Poker Champion Has a Simple Trick to Figure Out What Risks to Take—and Avoid," CNBC, August 30, 2022, https://www.cnbc.com/2022/08/30/top-poker-champion-dan-cates-simple-trick-for-risks-to-take-avoid.html.
22. Ibid.
23. Groeschel, *Think Ahead*, 110.
24. Cory Lee, Curb Free, https://curbfreewithcorylee.com/wheelchair-travel-blog/cory/.
25. Lisa Ann Pinkerton, "The Power of Influencer Marketing," PRSA, March 2022, https://www.prsa.org/article/the-power-of-influencer-marketing.
26. Groeschel, *Think Ahead*, 121.
27. "An Inspiring Example," Motivateus.com, https://motivateus.com/stories/example.htm.
28. Ibid.
29. Groeschel, *Think Ahead*, 139.

30. Mark Travers, "A Psychologist Tells You Why You Need to Escape the Toxic World of Self-Help," Forbes, https://www.forbes.com/sites/traversmark/2022/11/13/a-psychologist-tells-you-why-you-need-to-escape-the-toxic-world-of-self-help.

31. Ibid.

32. Alexandra Schwartz, "Improving Ourselves to Death," *The New Yorker*, January 8, 2018, https://www.new yorker.com/magazine/2018/01/15/improving-ourselves-to-death.

33. Groeschel, *Think Ahead*, 156.

34. Yield Giving, established by MacKenzie Scott, https://yieldgiving.com/.

35. Nicholas Kulish and Rebecca R. Ruiz, "The Fortunes of MacKenzie Scott," *The New York Times*, April 10, 2022, https://www.nytimes.com/2022/04/10/business/mackenzie-scott-charity.html.

36. Groeschel, *Think Ahead*, 168.

37. James Clear, *Atomic Habits* (New York: Avery/Penguin Random, 2018), 4.

38. Ibid, 7.

39. Groeschel, *Think Ahead*, 182.

40. Puja Roy, "How Many Times Thomas Failed? Know Edison's Marvellous and Lesser Known Inventions," Vedantu, November 22, 2022, https://www.vedantu.com/blog/how-many-times-edison-failed-to-invent-bulb.

41. Dr. Howard Markel, "The Day Marie Curie Got Snubbed by the French Science World," PBS News Hour, January 23, 2021, https://www.pbs.org/newshour/science/the-day-marie-curie-got-snubbed-by-the-french-science-world.

42. "Niels Bohr Biography," History-Biography, https://history-biography.com/niels-bohr/.

43. Groeschel, *Think Ahead*, 168.

44. Groeschel, *Think Ahead*, 182.

45. Jennifer Van Allen, "One Step at a Time," Runner's World, March 6, 2012, https://www.runnersworld.com/runners-stories/a20811594/one-step-at-a-time-0/.

46. Ibid.

MORE FROM
CRAIG GROESCHEL

ISBN 9780310151210

ISBN 9780310136828

AVAILABLE WHEREVER BOOKS ARE SOLD.

From the Publisher

GREAT STUDIES

ARE EVEN BETTER WHEN THEY'RE SHARED!

Help others find this study:

- Post a review at your favorite online bookseller.

- Post a picture on a social media account and share why you enjoyed it.

- Send a note to a friend who would also love it—or, better yet, go through it with them.

Thanks for helping others grow their faith!